JIMMY ARMFIELD

JIMMY ARMFIELD

THE OFFICAL BIOGRAPHY

ROY CALLEY

pitch

First published by Pitch Publishing, 2025

1

pitch

Pitch Publishing
9 Donnington Park,
85 Birdham Road,
Chichester, West Sussex,
PO20 7AJ

www.pitchpublishing.co.uk
info@pitchpublishing.co.uk

A CIP catalogue record is available for this book
from the British Library.

ISBN 978 1 83680 177 1

Typesetting and origination by Pitch Publishing

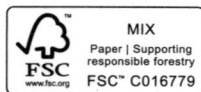

MIX
Paper | Supporting
responsible forestry
FSC
www.fsc.org   FSC™ C016779

Printed and bound on FSC® certified paper in line with
our continuing commitment to ethical business practices,
sustainability and the environment.

Printed and bound in India by Replika Press Pvt. Ltd.

Contents

Author's Foreword

HOW DO you write a biography? How do you structure something to tell the story of someone you admired so much? Do you start at the beginning and then follow it in a chronological timeline or maybe start at the peak of the person's career and achievements? It's always difficult and is made even more so in this instance because Jimmy Armfield was a man who was loved and admired in equal measure. Every person who knew him, met him or saw him play or listened to his words, will have a different view. There is no right or wrong way to honour a man who epitomised the 'beautiful game' long before that phrase became well worn.

The word 'legend' is used far too many times nowadays but if it had been a popular one when Jimmy was playing football, then he would have been described as just that. The almost original one-club man who could easily have played anywhere else and at a far greater and higher level than Blackpool, he encapsulated what is regarded as absent in today's modern game. Professionalism, fair play, loyalty and passion are words which sum up what Jimmy believed should be part of the life of a footballer.

Jimmy was a fine and dependable player in an era when flair and individuality were the norm as opposed to the exception.

He wasn't just a professional footballer, however. After his regrettably brief time as a manager, during which, naturally, he enjoyed success, he became one of the nation's most respected radio broadcasters, covering football matches for the BBC. This came from having developed a journalistic background and having the knowledge and experience to tell it the way it is. Sat alongside a firebrand commentator who had just described in excitable fashion *what* had just happened, Jimmy calmly explained exactly *how* it had happened. There was no one who came close to matching him in the role and it was at this point in my life that I met Jimmy properly, coming to regard him as a friend.

At the same time, he was working for the Football Association (FA), with one of his briefs to help find a new manager for the England national team – not once, but twice! Surely a difficult task for anyone, but Jimmy did it with all the professionalism you would expect. Each time, he got the nominations exactly right, even if on both occasions the final product wasn't quite what was advertised on the packaging.

The third part of Jimmy's life was that of a devoted family man and a stalwart supporter of the community of Blackpool. Never has anyone been as loyal to the town as him. When people talk of Blackpool, they naturally talk of the tower and the amusements and the beach, but when they talk of the football club (something which faded from fashion for many years), they talk of Matthews and Mortensen, but they talk of Armfield, too. It's sometimes quite incredible to remember that his weekends consisted of playing for Blackpool on a Saturday in the famous tangerine shirt at an exciting and glamourous setting, then playing the church organ for the congregation on a Sunday. If ever two lifestyles collided!

Jimmy was a great man and great is a word that is used far too many times, but it belongs to him and those who shared his values. He spent nearly a quarter of a century representing Blackpool and, of course, played for his country and yet he hardly won anything at either club or international level. When Blackpool lifted their first trophy in 18 years in 1971, the Anglo-Italian Cup, Jimmy had retired and when England lifted the Jules Rimet Trophy in 1966, he had been dropped by Alf Ramsey. Such are the vagaries of football.

In another universe, Jimmy would have been wearing the white away shirt of Manchester United on the day he retired and not the tangerine of Blackpool when the United players formed a guard of honour as he entered the Bloomfield Road arena. He would also have been stood tall alongside Bobby Moore, Geoff Hurst and fellow Blackpool man Alan Ball at Wembley, instead of sitting in the stands and watching. He showed no bitterness, though. Instead, he would just shrug, content in his belief that he had been fortunate to play the game at the highest level, a game that he loved and cared for. Not for him the public bitterness and recriminations over what others perceived as an injustice. He retained a quiet dignity in total keeping with the personality of a man who others grew to respect more and more. Former England manager Gareth Southgate used that story as inspiration when he told his players that *everyone* was important to the team as they built up to the Euro 2020 Final at Wembley. Jimmy didn't play in 1966 but he was as much a part of the team as the XI on the pitch. That was Jimmy. This is his story ...

Foreword by Glenn Hoddle

THE FIRST thing I have to say about Jimmy is that he was a true gentleman. In all of my dealings with him, he treated me with respect and loyalty. I remember when he first called me totally out of the blue about the England job. I was at Chelsea at the time, and I had no idea that Jimmy had targeted me to take over from Terry Venables. It was clear though, after we spoke and met a few times, that he was sure I was the right man for the job. I was excited and a little nervous, not really sure if it was the right time, but he reassured me.

Jimmy's loyalty also showed through when the press was becoming negative when there was a doubt we'd qualify for the 1998 World Cup. We'd lost 1-0 at home to Italy and had to play them in Rome, plus a tricky game against Georgia. I KNEW we'd qualify. I felt it, but the media weren't so sure. A few days later, Jimmy just calmly asked if I felt we'd make it to the finals in France, and I said yes. He just replied that my belief was good enough for him, and that was all I needed. Jimmy was an ally, and of course we did qualify.

We never quite knew exactly what Jimmy's role was at the FA, but he was a calm voice. He had his opinions, but he never forced them on us. I was left alone to do the job, and I appreciated that. When I found myself in the eye of the storm of the media when I left the position, I always felt that Jimmy was there supporting me. Unfortunately, he wasn't in a powerful enough position to change things. It was sad, because we had a great team at the time, and it was clear we were going to go far, but the media had other ideas.

In later years I listened to Jimmy on the radio. You didn't even have to have him introduced, because that voice was so recognisable. Knowledgeable, calm, understanding of the game and clear in the way he explained things.

'Gentleman Jim' has been used to describe him, and I can't think of a better compliment. He was so good to me, and I am always grateful that I was fortunate to have met him.

Foreword by Duncan Armfield

FREQUENTLY MY BROTHER and I read and listen to many things about dad. To us, he was just that … dad. Day to day, nothing ever seemed out of the ordinary and our family life with our mother and grandparents was as happy as anyone could wish for, filled with love and time spent together. Therefore, we knew that the family was the rock we had our lives built upon. We were so lucky.

Yet, in all of this, extraordinary events would regularly happen. As we grew older and understood better, it dawns on you that in all the family normality, there was this thing of football. Family friends, such as Bobby Charlton, were in fact the superstars of the day. Being taken to Leeds United and sitting in the players' lounge watching TV with Bremner, Giles, Clarke, Madeley, Gray, Hunter and the rest of that fabulous title-winning team. Your father running out as captain of Blackpool Football Club in his tangerine shirt with the white number 2, in front of the fans he adored playing for. Dad shouting to mum 'I am just off to have a cup of tea with the maestro [Sir Stanley Matthews] and see how he is.'

In any biography about a dad, the family wants to ensure as much accuracy as is possible. When Roy asked to have the eulogy we gave for Dad at his funeral, we accepted, and you can read for yourself the father we knew and miss. The words came straight from the heart, and although we were grieving, you can see it was full of this wonderful man's impact on us and the world around him. We knew we had to share him, and so many people saw him as a friend. Even if it was after one brief conversation, because he gave you his full attention, listened and gave that most precious gift of time for you. Dad was a man of the people and was often described as Mr Blackpool because he was so down to earth. He kept our feet firmly on the ground as a family and taught us respect for our fellow man and to be kind.

Dad's life was happy, and he took every opportunity offered to him, after careful consideration at times. His parents were hard-working, both being employed well past the normal retirement age, which provided that ethic and mantra in his life. He always said we Armfields are grafters, because although opportunities appear, he told us, you have to work hard and get things done to make it a success. He would stay behind at training to refine his skills and even after football he would keep fit and look after himself, even giving up his beloved pipe aged 57. He worked hard to be a journalist and broadcaster, taking elocution lessons to ensure he could be understood by the listeners to Radio 5. On his coat of arms, given to him for being Lord High Sheriff of Lancashire, is the word persevere, and he certainly did.

Although we miss him, reflections on Dad from books like this can keep his name alive, which helps us as a family and others who did not know him so well. He always said that life was for the living, and generally change was good. Looking back can sometimes give distorted pictures of how the world was better and simpler, and sometimes it was. Yet Dad was a fan of progress and in the book you can see how he put that into practice.

Most of all he was just a thoroughly good man. A gentleman and a gentle man. Gentleman Jim. Never publicly critical, seeing the best, enthusiastic, passionate, kind, thoughtful, loyal and brilliant to be with. Full of stories, jokes and good advice. Eloquent, calm, motivational, knowledgeable, experienced and loving. No wonder we are so proud he was our dad.

Chapter One:

The beginning

ON 13 May 1959, Jimmy Armfield was stood on the pitch at the Maracanã Stadium in Rio de Janeiro wearing an England shirt. Around him were 160,000 Brazilian supporters who had been showered from above by leaflets from political activists, meaning their frenzied-like fervour was on the verge of becoming unmanageable. Riot police circled the pitch whilst loudspeakers rang with the sounds of propaganda songs and the Brazilian national anthem. There was a lengthy delay before kick-off and the England team were nervous and overwhelmed. Jimmy was making his debut for his national side. He was 23 years of age. One can only imagine his thoughts, his fears and his excitement.

There's a lot to fill in from the moment Jimmy entered the world up to that Wednesday afternoon in the South American cauldron. A lot to digest and to savour, as the baby boy grew into a strapping young man who seemed to excel at sport almost immediately. When Christopher and Doris gazed at their newborn on that Saturday, 21 September 1935 (and that's something that was never lost on Jimmy – the fact that it was a Saturday), could there have ever been a moment when they could have imagined how his life would work out?

It was the 1930s. Britain was in that curious state of affairs that can only be imagined at now. The country was still suffering the mental and physical hangover of the terrible First World War, knowing deep down that the threat from Chancellor Hitler was becoming greater and greater as each week passed, with a second conflict seeming an inevitability. It was a calm Britain, though, almost completely devoid of the cars, the commercialism and the American influence; a Britain where the horse-drawn carriage still worked in the rural countryside, but a nation still riddled with a rigid class system that was born and bred in the United Kingdom. Jimmy was most definitely born into a working-class family and those values that so define the people of that time could be seen throughout his life, both as a professional and a gentleman. It was what was expected.

He was brought up initially in an area called Denton, in those days a separate suburb but now completely encased in the city of Manchester. The family lived in a 'two up, two down', as it was charmingly called. It was a house without electricity and with a gas supply that needed a few pennies to top it up on a daily basis. Like all working-class families who have little, the Armfields prided themselves on their cleanliness and godliness, and the house was never a place for slovenly behaviour. Again, it's another impression that stayed with Jimmy, as there was never a time when he would be seen publicly dressed in a less than smart way. Clothes maketh the man. Jimmy was smart, both in attire and in intellect. The godliness was there from the very beginning.

Father worked in a grocer's store in the Co-op, Mother was at home keeping the house. For six days a week, Christopher would accept the back-breaking lifting and heaving of heavy sugar bags in a cellar, sweating and aching, whilst Doris made a point of keeping the young Jimmy on the right road to happiness. A deep belief in God knitted the family together and this strong faith kept Jimmy company throughout his life. It was what working-class people did. Whilst the politicians and the businessmen and the lords and the earls all took care of a country that was feeling the effects of the crumbling Empire, the families in their small, identical houses worked and accepted their lot. There was little chance of advancement but there was always time for happiness. It was a time of tension and there was no guaranteed future for anyone, so each day was lived in a way that would not register today. It was a world that bears little resemblance to the times we live in, with life in the north of England defined by soot-blackened buildings, rattling trams that pondered along the grey streets and a trip to the picture house being the highlight of a deadening week. Life was so different.

How did James Christopher Armfield get to know the game of football in those seemingly dark and depressing days? He was born at a time when the game was almost completely the preserve of the working man, so avoiding it would be an impossibility. Was he like all the children of the age, immortalised in grainy black-and-white photos, where raggedy backstreets played host to Manchester City against the Arsenal? Where the white paint on the walls signified the goal and where a bare tennis ball was used as the football that honed a thousand skills? In those days, nearly every young lad wanted to be 'Dixie' Dean or maybe Peter Doherty or, if you knew Blackpool, then it was Jimmy Hampson. Football was on a par with cricket for popularity, whilst the other sport that nearly captured our hero, rugby, was enjoying a healthy renaissance. Having said that, Jimmy was only four years of age when the Second World War broke out, so his introduction to the delights of the national game would have been delayed and also overshadowed by the threat from above.

Getting to know the game of football (or soccer as it was still widely known as in the 1930s) in a period of anxiety and poverty was not a thing of the moment. The radio, or wireless, and the local newspapers were the only available sources of knowledge. Footballers weren't personalities. No one knew what they looked like. Clubs weren't community assets. The era of 'Super Sunday', where each game of top-tier football has to be bigger and better than the last game of top-tier football, was so far away it could have belonged to a different world. There was no connection between the game and money, or the game and celebrity status, or even the game and news headlines. Games of football were played out to a local audience, where the trickle of information took its time to reach those who couldn't attend. A result didn't resonate around the country but caused a minor stir in the households and the public houses over a pint of mild. Football matches were the entertainment of a Saturday afternoon on terraces that stretched as far as the eye could see, with the air permeated with the aroma of Brylcreem and Woodbines, mixed with the unmistakable smell of Bovril. Club chairmen owned cotton mills and drove Bentley cars. Men wore flat caps, women stayed at home.

Jimmy grew up at a school which encouraged physical sports, but then most of them did. The government of the time had implemented a strict physical fitness regime for youngsters, knowing that one day they would need to call upon them in a time of conflict. That time was fast approaching. This was the era in which 'Gentleman Jim' was brought up. This was the time that forged the man and the professional footballer. This was the time that we should explore more before continuing.

The 'nation of shopkeepers', as Great Britain had been described a century earlier, was now, more than ever, living up to that title. Small businesses abounded as unemployment was rife, especially amongst the working-classes. Butchers, bakers, candlestick makers were all in abundance as the government embarked on a city rejuvenation project to destroy the slums that blighted the larger areas and make affordable housing for all. Unfortunately, the advent of the second major world conflict brought such lofty ambitions to an end.

As war was declared, the cry went out to evacuate the children from areas of danger and, although Manchester was not regarded as particularly unsafe at the start of the war, despite a blitz in the first couple of years, Jimmy's mother clearly had her concerns, as it was she who made the decision to move her little Jimmy away from the soot-grimed streets of Manchester to the clean and purer air of Blackpool.

Blackpool. The town immortalised in the morale-boosting depression film *Sing As We Go* featuring Gracie Fields, was the place to aspire to. It was the holiday getaway of a lifetime. It represented the lightness away from the mills and the mines and the factories. Blackpool offered fantasy when the country was fog-bound in a nightmare. Who could resist it?

At the time, Jimmy was 'about seven', according to his autobiography *Right Back to the Beginning*, and he had absolutely no idea why Blackpool was chosen. Having said that, it probably wasn't too difficult to guess. At least his mother had the means to make it happen. All he remembered was leaving school one day, catching a bus to Victoria Station with her and then a train to Blackpool, which in those days was not an easy task. He arrived at North Station in a pair of short trousers and a cap and opened his eyes wide to a paradise setting. Blackpool was different. Blackpool was a popular seaside resort. Blackpool now had Jimmy in its grasp and it never let go.

He did try to break that grasp, though, if only temporarily. Notably the time he rode his bicycle to Denton and back, with little clue as to the direction, a journey that took up to five hours. He went to visit his father – who was suitably shocked and impressed at the same time – stayed for an hour and then rode back again. It was a different time. Jimmy would have had the same opportunity of catching either a bus or train to Denton as we might of taking a space shuttle today. The public transport was a working-class invention but was beyond the means of those very same people it promised to serve.

The bond, though, between Jimmy, a young and excitable child who had the seven miles of sand at his disposal, and Blackpool was forged from the moment he arrived and that connection stayed with him all of his life. In those days, Blackpool wasn't the brash and vulgar place that it portrays today, with its stag nights and hen dos. It was different. It had class and was an escape for the mill workers, the miners and the poor, who came in their thousands to enjoy the beach, the candy floss and the ice cream. A ride on a donkey on the sands was an adventure rarely experienced and a trip up the tower was only for the brave. Blackpool was an escape, especially in the heart of the conflict, and Jimmy had this on his doorstep each and every day. Even the absence, initially, of his father, who would visit on weekends, was countered by a walk with his mother on the breezy promenade, with a weekend treat of a trip to the Pleasure Beach and its rollercoasters and laughing clown. Life was better now.

He and his mother lived on the top floor of a boarding house that welcomed soldiers and those down on their luck. It was a small room with a shared bathroom and it seems that Jimmy's one bath a week rule was flouted regularly, as he was a constant visitor to the local swimming pool and enjoyed the delights of the Irish Sea, even in the cold. He started school at Revoe, a well-known learning place even then, but it didn't hold him too many times. Truancy was a feature for a curious young boy, who found the stuffiness of the classroom inhibiting and, anyway, he wanted to play sport. He did, however, become a successful student once he'd settled down and the school always kept a fond place in his heart.

His introduction to football came at the ground that he ultimately graced as a player for nearly 20 years, Bloomfield Road. One of the Polish soldiers who rented a room in the boarding house where the Armfields lived was a football fanatic and took Jimmy to his first game. He could hardly have appreciated the Pandora's box that visit was about to open up. Poland can't claim to often have been at the forefront of the game down the years but introducing Jimmy Armfield to it is something worth savouring.

Blackpool were on the verge of greatness when the war broke out, sitting comfortably at the top of the First Division (admittedly after only three games played) and were regarded as one of the strongest teams in England. The war didn't really change that, as thousands of servicemen were stationed in the town and a fair few played football.

The town was never bombed and it was said that Hitler had actually made a point of keeping it from harm's way as he saw it as the entertainment capital that would amuse the German people once his planned occupation was achieved. One can only imagine and shudder at what a German-occupied Blackpool would look like. Whatever the truth of Hitler's knowledge of Blackpool, it was safe and American, Polish and, of course, many British soldiers found themselves in the seaside town, with all of its attractions, football being one of them.

Bloomfield Road was requisitioned by the military during the war (which helped to pay the rent for the club, too) but games were played on a regular basis and the team was so successful that it became a huge draw for those looking for cheap entertainment. They actually won the War Cup and, although it was a challenge tournament involving only four teams, their 4-2 win at Stamford Bridge against Arsenal was regarded as one of the best performances ever produced by an English team. The almost amusing side story of that victory is that the Arsenal team were so confident of a win that they had a photograph of themselves with the trophy taken before the game was played! Not only that, but they never handed it to Blackpool anyway, so the War Cup has never graced the rather bare trophy cabinet at Bloomfield Road.

It was hardly surprising that Jimmy wanted to be part of the 'tangerine dream' (well before the term was used), as the club had started to climb the hill that led to the heights of success. Watching Mortensen, Dodds and, occasionally, Matthews must have had an enlightening effect on the young boy, who was now reaching his tenth birthday. Harry Johnston was another idol and, in one of those quirks of fate, it was Harry's parents who took Jimmy's parents to Blackpool for the first time for a day out. Such things life is made of.

Boys' kickabouts under the streetlights now involved Blackpool against the Arsenal, as they were the 'coming' team. It may have been a virtually different set of players who ran out wearing the tangerine shirts in those days of watching under gloomy skies but, due to the number of footballers available in the area, Blackpool had the pick of the best. Watching 'Jock' Dodds scoring six, seven and eight goals per game at times must have had a huge impression on Jimmy, yet his dreams of playing as a goalscorer changed many years later.

Whilst the war raged on in foreign lands and the bombs fell many miles away, Jimmy took hold of his favourite possession, a well-worn tennis ball, and, like so many others, honed his football skills. He was a young lad, blissfully unaware of the conflict that was tearing the world apart. Blackpool was effectively untouched, apart from the huge posts that were buried deep into the sands on the beach, a counter to any enemy aircraft trying to land. It was doubtful that the Germans would actually get that far north with their raids, but Blackpool played its part in being prepared for such an event. What the town did share with the rest of the country, though, was the daily struggle to get enough food. Rationing was, of course, the only way of making sure every citizen had enough to eat but it dominated the minds and thoughts of the housewife who each day had to queue and hope that the last sausage or lump of cheese or loaf of bread was still on the shelf when she got to the front. Jimmy later put his ailments down to the fact that he never really had enough to eat when he was a child. Small wonder that he ended up being as fit as he was.

It wasn't just football, though, that attracted this young athlete. At the age of ten, the war was now over and Jimmy was passionate about football, played rugby union for Arnold School and also batted and bowled to a reasonable degree in cricket. Added to that, he was a very fast runner and would regularly pick up trophies for his speed at school sports days. Any of these activities could have ensnared him but it was football that won … and there was never a doubt.

It's worth taking a pause here to imagine what it would have been like not having Jimmy Armfield as a footballer. He was big and strong enough to play rugby and you can really imagine him running down the flanks in a Calcutta Cup game against Scotland at Twickenham. Equally, you can see in your mind's eye him sweeping the ball past square leg and to the boundary in cricket, but could you see him in a 100-yard dash? He was fast but it just doesn't look or feel right. No, Jimmy was a footballer. It was ordained.

Jimmy said that he didn't grow up supporting a team. It wasn't really possible during the Second World War, as the leagues were run on an ad hoc basis and it was difficult identifying with different players each week, but he grew up supporting football. As he lived in Blackpool, it was natural that his allegiance was there. None of his family were particularly sporting and it does seem that Jimmy was the exception rather than the rule in the Armfield clan, but what an exception he became.

How did he start his professional footballing career? It's a long story and there's so much to fill in, but we'll start with the one man, and the one event, that was instrumental in his development. The return of his father.

After the war ended, his father joined the family in Blackpool and, after a brief period of living in separate rooms, they finally became one when he rented a small shop complete with upstairs living accommodation. It was hardly luxurious and was in a part of town that can still only be described as rough. Blackpool has always had a reputation and the years after the war were no different to today. There was a pub next door where there would be gangland fights, drunken brawls and the kind of moments that few youngsters of Jimmy's age would witness, but the accommodation above the shop was home and he had his own room.

His father took a dim view of Jimmy's casual attitude to school attendance and, with his mother, made sure that there were to be no more days of truancy, no more misbehaving and a desire to make the best of his life. The image of a trouble-making young Jimmy is at odds with his later persona, but the child becomes a man and it's at that time that his direction is shown. All parents want the same for their children but it seemed to be of even more importance at that time, especially if the spectre of poverty hovered above on a daily basis. The Armfields were never poor but every penny was worked for and every penny was accounted for. Making sure that every morsel on the plate was finished at mealtimes was an effective way of making the child appreciate the value of life.

The grocer's shop his father ran was, at times, hit and miss with its trade, always reliant on the booming tourist trade that Blackpool was becoming famous for. Mother got herself a part-time evening job, too, working in a refreshment stall on Central Pier, where she served the stars with cups of tea and a kind word for those down on their luck. Jimmy, too, was involved in helping the family survive, taking the bread round on his bike, cycling the cobbled streets of the town and receiving an occasional sixpence from a thankful customer.

It was at this time that his education took on a more serious note, with the move to Arnold School after his 11-plus, and that his faith became imprinted on his mind. Like all children of his age in that era, he attended a Sunday school, this one being at a Methodist church in the town. As a youngster, it probably just meant a trip to see friends and have fun, despite the restrictions of having to wear their 'Sunday best'. There were japes and mischiefs but nothing that any other child hadn't done before, yet his father wasn't allowing that to continue. A disciplinarian, but a kind one at that.

Kindness was probably not the way that Jimmy may have described his father after returning home with a bad mark on his daily school report. He'd struggled with his lessons and his father decided the best way to instil a harder working attitude in his wayward son was to give him a slap around the head and then speak to the headmaster. The next morning, Jimmy was summoned to the headmaster's office, all lacquered wood and ornate portraits, where Frank Holdgate, the headmaster in question, announced that Jimmy would have to spend the next Saturday afternoon in the school writing an essay. It didn't matter that Blackpool were playing Fulham at Bloomfield Road in an FA Cup tie, Jimmy would be in the classroom.

After one seemingly innocent incident (certainly when viewed from the perspective of the third decade of this century) in which he apparently deliberately sang the wrong words to a hymn, his father took him to the nearest Sunday school to their home. It was St Peter's Church and he announced to a clearly shocked Jimmy that this was to be his new place of attendance, breaking the ties with the friends and his 'partners-in-crime' of the past. It obviously worked, as right up until his death, Jimmy continued to be involved at St Peter's. He became an Anglican and relied on his faith, born and honed in the cloisters, throughout his life. It helped with his life choices and it helped with his football, which now we will address.

Chapter Two:

Do you want to play for Blackpool?

IT'S DIFFICULT to comprehend today how much of an attraction Blackpool, and indeed Blackpool Football Club, were in the days, months and years immediately after the war. Britain was a nation that, despite victory, was on its knees financially and spiritually, was a nation that had stood proudly alone against the seemingly inevitable onset of Nazi power and was a nation that finally had to almost bankrupt itself as its major ally helped it win a war that had killed so many. There had to be a respite, a way of forgetting, a way of letting your hair down and forgetting the belief that you only had to live for the day. There was a future and this is where Blackpool came in.

The seaside town, now gaudy and the almost inclusive environ of the drunken lads' night out or the girls in skimpy clothing was, in 1945, a paradise that was far away from the bunkers, the bombed-out buildings and the slums that had multiplied during the hostilities. Its fresh air, its miles of golden sands, the tower that stretched into the sky as far as the eye could see, the piers with their candyfloss, toffee apples and windswept girls. It was heaven and Britain needed a heaven.

The football club had always been a passing distraction, never really offering anything more than a local celebration as a promotion was gained or a cup tie won. Their most famous player, the prolific Jimmy Hampson, had died in a fishing accident off Fleetwood Bay in 1938, his body never found. The town mourned a man who had scored nearly 250 goals in a Blackpool shirt, but elsewhere it was a statistic lost in time. Then came the war.

Blackpool actually led the First Division when Prime Minister Neville Chamberlain declared war on Germany. They'd played three games and won all three. Manager Joe Smith was on the verge of creating one of the most attacking and entertaining football sides ever seen in England and it seemed that success was in their grasp. The war didn't stop that.

As more and more soldiers were billeted in Blackpool, far away from the bombs and the night raids, there came among them talented footballers who wanted to continue playing during their time at home. The list is almost endless, but Stanley Matthews made his first appearance for Blackpool during the war, as did Jock Dodds, Hugh Kelly and Tommy Garrett. With these and other guest players, the team were now a force in English football. The Bloomfield Road ground was kept open as it was requisitioned by the RAF, so games could be played in front of larger and larger crowds, with Blackpool Football Club becoming one of the biggest clubs in the country. If the word glamorous was used in those times, then Blackpool would have been described as a glamorous club. The 1943 War Cup Final victory against Arsenal at Stamford Bridge was described by the *Daily Mail* as 'one of the greatest performances by a football team in the country', which is some praise indeed. It was this that Jimmy grew up amongst. This was the club he obviously wanted to play for and this was the club he was to spend the whole of his footballing-playing career at. How did it happen though?

Jimmy was a runner. He was fast. All of his life he ran. It made him feel better if there were problems. At school, that pace helped on the football field, where he played up front as a striker, but it also helped in his second chosen sport of rugby union and when he played cricket, especially out in the field. At one stage, it looked like rugby would get its man. His teacher pursued him to take up the game on a more full-time basis but, in the end, the lure of football was far too much for Jimmy and he started playing for his Sunday school team.

Like all youngsters of his age at that time, his football field was the street he lived on, empty of motorised transport but full of personal dreams. His football was the bare tennis ball that he kept lovingly and his crowd were the women scrubbing the front doorsteps. It's how so many of the footballing greats down the years started and Jimmy was no exception. He told the story of how his Sunday school team played a Tyldesley Youth Club team and were outnumbered by them on the pitch by 11 to 7. They were also outnumbered by them by about 20 goals, too. On the opposite side was a player by the name of Brian Harper who, in later years, became 'The Blackpool Rock' as he boxed under the ring name Brian London and had two unsuccessful challenges for the world heavyweight title against Floyd Patterson and Muhammad Ali.

It was at the age of 15 that Jimmy was suddenly introduced to the football club he had been supporting during the years after the war. It was 1951 and Blackpool had made a second appearance at Wembley in the FA Cup Final, although they had lost timidly to a Newcastle United team in its pomp. In 1948, they'd played against Manchester United and lost 4-2. It was regarded as one of the best footballing finals ever seen at the stadium but Blackpool had somehow thrown away what was looking like a certain victory. Against Newcastle, they didn't turn up and the Blackpool team returned to Lancashire deadened and beaten.

The club weren't in any type of crisis and, indeed, younger supporters of Blackpool would define the word in a far more dramatic way, but they did reach out to the community in a bid to bolster their ranks. The call had gone out to schools and youth clubs for decent young lads who had potential, and Jimmy's PT master, George Neal, had put his name forward. Only now can that decision be seen in all of its importance. At the time, Jimmy was just another young lad who had a flair for the game. Such moments are lives made of.

The story of the trial day, which was the following Friday, seems to be one of complete chaos. They weren't expecting him, they had no idea what position he played in (but then neither did Jimmy, apparently) and the teams were randomly picked. Jimmy said he would play on the wing. It worked. His team won 4-1 and he scored all four! He was immediately asked to play for the Blackpool Colts first team but he declined. An astonishing decision? Today, it seems that way but, at the time, his loyalty was to his school and they needed him to play football *and* rugby right up to the end of term. He couldn't go against the wishes of his school. There was no choice.

Thankfully, the story didn't end there. If it had, you wouldn't be reading this now. Jimmy was invited back to the club during the summer (Blackpool must have wondered who this precocious young lad was and how brazen it was to turn down the opportunity) and, after a successful trial where he felt convinced they had no idea who he was, he was signed on for Blackpool Colts. History was in the making, not that anyone knew it at that time. Home games were played at Bispham Education ground, some miles from Bloomfield Road, and mostly it was a case of a boy (Jimmy, at the age of 16) playing against men. However, he did make the local newspaper after scoring two goals in a victory, so the name Jimmy Armfield had already registered.

Promotion came with the move to the Blackpool 'A' team, who played in the Lancashire League. Opponents were Preston North End, Blackburn Rovers, Burnley and Bolton Wanderers (at a time when Bolton was stuck firmly in the county of Lancashire). This, even today. sounds like a dream for any self-respecting Blackpool fan. It was steady progress for Jimmy, who was playing well but not really making headlines. That is, until one moment changed his life forever. It sounds melodramatic but it was another event that shaped the player he became.

He was playing at Bloomfield Road in front of a sparse crowd and those who were there had their minds and interests elsewhere. At the same time, the first team were at Villa Park beating Tottenham Hotspur in an FA Cup semi-final and many supporters at Bloomfield Road had wireless radios with them to listen to the commentary. Could this be the season that 'Our Stan' (Matthews) would finally win his FA Cup winners' medal? It seemed incredible that a player of his age (38) should be in that position again and the drama being played out in Birmingham was far more interesting to those at Bloomfield Road than what was being played out in front of them. Then the right-back in Jimmy's team was injured and the story goes ...

> There were no substitutions allowed in those days and Vince (McKenna, the manager) was wondering what to do, so I volunteered to play right-back and right-wing combined. I said I would be a wing-back. It was the first time I'd played at the back and I remember thinking how much easier it was than being up there in the frontline. It seemed so natural for me to be there and, from that point, I never really played anywhere else.

Those words came from Jimmy's autobiography, *Right Back to the Beginning*, and show how such a simple moment in a person's life can transform it in a dramatic way. Jimmy was now a full-back. The position that can never be associated with anyone else at Blackpool and, to a certain extent, with England, too. He took the right-back role to another sphere but we are getting ahead of ourselves. Blackpool had made it to Wembley for the third time, for the 1953 FA Cup Final, and a young Jimmy Armfield had changed positions on a football pitch. One event seemed innocuous, whilst the other led to a drama that was as dramatic as dramatic can be.

Jimmy's debut in the reserve team came shortly afterwards but let's just pause and breathe, because even this moment is worth savouring. In today's game, a player can be 'fatigued' or 'not in the right state of mind' to play for his team. Usually, it's a high-profile player with a very high-profile lifestyle complete with all the financial trappings available to anyone who can play the game at a very competitive level. Jimmy was certainly talented enough to make that level but this was a different era, a different time and a different mindset. Jimmy made his debut for the reserve side of one of the strongest teams in England just *hours* after playing in the youth team for the same club. Yes, *two* games in one day. This type of commitment would be totally lost on the majority of modern-day footballers but Jimmy Armfield played at right-back against Leeds United in the morning and then played in the same position against Bury in the afternoon. One was a youth game, the next a reserve match. It is almost impossible to believe and what makes it even more incredible is that Jimmy actually bemoans missing a 'sitter' late in the Bury game because he was too excited! Oh, and in between the matches he'd run home to tell his dad, had a quick sandwich and then run to the ground for the second game.

Jimmy got his reward, though; not that he needed anything else apart from wearing the now-famous tangerine shirt. Even though he still hadn't signed professional terms, he went to Wembley for the 1953 FA Cup Final and witnessed history. It was actually his third visit to the old stadium, as he'd been to the two previous Blackpool finals, but this was different. Witnessing one of the greatest comebacks in a cup final, Stan Mortensen scoring a hat-trick and the love that followed the legendary Stanley Matthews, it was one of those times when you probably knew that history was being made. Only those who stood there on the terraces of the colossal stadium could appreciate what they were witnessing. Even though, with live football on television still in its infancy, the match was shown live, the pictures were grainy and jumpy, and the sound was intermittent. You had to be there and Jimmy was. He even got a photograph with the trophy two days later. Sadly, Blackpool and Jimmy's association with that famous tournament was, from then onwards, a fleeting affair. They certainly never got close to touching the trophy again.

Matthews, Mortensen, Johnston and co. returned to the town as heroes, the promenade full of supporters, the town hall decorated in ceremonial style. Matthews made his famous 'there were 11 players' speech, engraved cigarette lighters were given to the team and the television cameras got in everyone's way. The latter weren't to return for many more years. Blackpool had won the FA Cup. They were famous. Matthews had his medal. Morty had scored a hat-trick. Was there a better place to be in England at that time?

Maybe the excitement of the FA Cup success was the final reckoning for Jimmy? He loved football but he was still playing rugby for his school. His father had a different future mapped out for him, as so many parents have, especially as Jimmy was proving something of a success academically. He'd passed his A levels in history, geography and economics and was accepted by both Liverpool University and Loughborough College, so his future seemed determined, but this was the making of the man that Jimmy had become. He *knew* his future was with 'the beautiful game' far earlier than when it was first described as such. He had a passion for football. He played it, he dreamt it, he watched it, he read about it and he knew it. Jimmy Armfield would not be in the city or in the offices of a bank or in a team of accountants. Jimmy would be a footballer. So, when the time came, he told his father of his plans and waited.

This should be a moment where we read of his father's displeasure, the harsh words that followed and the general disappointment that he felt over his son's decision; a moment that clouded their relationship until the day his father died, but it isn't. His father was quiet. He listened and he nodded, and then he told Jimmy in firm but understanding tones that it 'was his life … you have to lead it … make decisions and stand by them'.

As Jimmy always stated, his father was the best anyone could have hoped for and the support he received from his parents was a true product of love and care, something Jimmy was to show many times to his own children down the years. As Duncan, Jimmy's son, reflected:

> He was just a fantastic father. He did everything for us. He said never to worry. Don't worry about money, because he would always provide. He taught us the values we hold dear today. He was always there for us.

Before Jimmy could take up his love of football, there was, and it was inevitable in the time he lived, an army call-up. National Service, the two words that would inspire fear and trepidation in the youngsters of today, was all part of growing up in the England of the 1950s and Jimmy had to serve his time. There was no alternative. He had no choice. No one did. Whatever life path that was being trod, it had to be set aside for two years whilst the government-backed army took a spotty-faced youngster and made him into a man. Whether that type of transformation would be possible in today's world is a matter for amusing conjecture but, in the 1950s, it was the life they led.

Chapter Three:

You're in the army now …

JIMMY WAS becoming an established player at Blackpool. Well, established in that he was breaking through to the reserve team and the people who mattered were taking notice. He was still on amateur forms in 1954 when he fully left school and, with hindsight, there could be an obvious reason why the club kept it that way. They knew, and Jimmy knew, that his National Service papers would soon be served. To be fair to Blackpool – and, let's be honest, the club has never had a reputation for paying money that wasn't absolutely necessary – they did sign Jimmy on temporary professional terms of £1 per week, with a promise of £7 if he made the first team. There was also the promise that he would receive full terms and become a professional once his time in the army had ended but these were fragile and worrying times for the country. Britain was a nation still recovering and paying for a war it had won. Economic benefits were lost on most and the poverty that strangled society at that time was all too evident. Jimmy wasn't in poverty but it was a time when few knew where the next wage may come from. Footballers were not immune to the vagaries of a society that was struggling to put food on the table.

Being in the army, though, at least gave a sense of security and, with Jimmy's ability to self-discipline, it didn't seem as burdensome as others may have found it. Dumped into the King's Own Royal Regiment in Lancaster, he soon found that being part of the army was hardly a glamorous pursuit. There was the predictable boot-cleaning (something he was probably more familiar with than most), parade-stomping and the general unpleasantness that could be associated with military service.

If Jimmy thought he'd be able to continue his Blackpool footballing career whilst there, he was to receive an immediate shock. For the first month, he was barracked in a room that he described as being unchanged since the Boer War and that was it. He was shown how to use a rifle, a possession that was so important in the army that there could be serious consequences if it was lost or even damaged, and he was taught the comradeship and loyalty that so defined his personality for the rest of his life. Loyalty, in particular, is a word that sums up Jimmy Armfield and it's a subject we will return to on many occasions throughout this biography.

Football was there, though. Football was always there and very soon it became clear in the kickabout games that there was something special about Lance Corporal Armfield and so, within two weeks, he was promoted to the regimental team. This didn't just coincide with but actually resulted in them winning the North-West District League two years running, something they had failed to do for a very, very long time.

Football continued to be there and when he was given the opportunity of attending an officer's course, Jimmy firmly refused the invitation. He wanted to be a footballer and had no interest at all in continuing his career in the army once his service had been completed. It was a brave and rather unpopular decision, which must have caused a few strained moments with his superiors, but the young man knew his destiny. For those who accused him in later life of being indecisive, especially as manager of Leeds United, then this was a Jimmy Armfield who knew how to make a decision and then stand by it.

For that reason, Jimmy stayed in England when the rest of the regiment were posted to Hong Kong. As he said: 'I went to Hong Kong much later in my life, and it probably looked better from my hotel room.' So, he stayed and took on the role of a PT instructor. It also gave him the opportunity of returning to Blackpool at the weekends and picking up his career there, as the reserve team were pretty desperate to have him back. He started to make an impression and soon it was clear that a first-team opportunity wouldn't be that far away. When it came, it came as a surprise to Jimmy and the team!

By the Christmas of 1954, Blackpool were still regarded as one of the best teams in the country. They'd relinquished their hold on the FA Cup in a pretty timid fashion to Third Division Port Vale but they still had Matthews, Mortensen and Johnston and they'd finished in sixth position in the First Division to back up the cup success. Joe Smith was still building and rebuilding the team and the Bloomfield Road ground was still packed to capacity for virtually every game. It was in this sphere of constant success that Jimmy Armfield made his first-team debut for Blackpool and the first of his 627 appearances for the club. This moment deserves more than just an addition to a paragraph.

The start

It was Monday, 27 December 1954. It was Fratton Park against a Portsmouth side who were to finish third in the league. Blackpool were having a season to forget, thankfully dodging relegation by three points after only winning 14 of their 42 league games. Few of the 43,000 spectators on that day would have imagined that the young full-back making his rather unremarkable debut would go on to play for England at the highest level and captain his national side, too. Even the build-up to such a major event was underwhelming, as Jimmy explains in his biography:

> Blackpool were due to play Portsmouth on Christmas Day morning with the reverse game at Fratton Park on the Monday. I went to the Christmas match, which finished 2-2, and I was still in bed the next morning when the phone rang downstairs. My father took the call in the shop and hurried upstairs, saying "You're wanted on the phone. It's the manager, Joe Smith". I ran down the stairs and picked up the phone. Joe said 'We've got an injury or two. We want you down at Portsmouth. Will you be all right?'

That was it. No fanfare. No press conferences. No discussions. There was an injury and Jimmy was wanted. It didn't matter that he was in Blackpool, had little idea as to how to get to the south coast or the fact that he had to be back in the barracks in Lancaster on the Tuesday evening. This was Jimmy's chance!

One can only imagine what was going through his mind at that time. At the tender age of 19, he had already served a portion of his National Service and was making a good impression in the Blackpool reserve side, as well as numerous army teams, but this was the big one. All of his dreams and aspirations were about to come true. The players he had watched, such as Matthews and Mortensen and Johnston, were to be his team-mates (although the first two were actually injured for that match), even if it was only to last for one match. Jimmy Armfield was about to play in the tangerine shirt for the first team of Blackpool Football Club, something which cannot be overstated today. This club, despite its problems that season, was still one of the biggest draws in England. This was Blackpool. Today, you might be able to say 'this was Chelsea or this was Spurs', which shows the magnitude of the popularity of the club. It was a big moment but the problem was, how on earth to get there and back in time!

In today's modern footballing world, a manager will bemoan the fact that his players have had to play twice in four days and will regularly field an under-strength side for a competition that isn't regarded as important. Not in the 1950s. Playing on Christmas Day was accepted and playing two days later, some 300 miles away to the same team, was a curiosity that defies understanding today. After all, there were no motorways and internal flights weren't exactly a regular option, so how did he do it? How did any of them do it?

Well, later that day, he caught a bus to Preston, where he met up with the team and they then took the train down to London Euston. A bus then took them to a hotel called The Grand, which, according to Jimmy, was anything but. He had to share a room and Jimmy admits that, during the hotel stay, he hardly said a word and kept himself to himself, especially as none of the team knew who he was. The next morning, it was a bus to London Waterloo, then a train to Portsmouth, where they enjoyed the delights of the dining carriage, before yet another bus took them to the ground. It's hardly surprising that within 25 minutes of kick-off, they were 3-0 down, with Jimmy having barely touched the ball. As he recounted later in his life in an exclusive interview with BBC Radio 5 Live:

> When we reached the dressing room, I was told I would be playing at right-back. I sat down, started to change and I don't think I said a word before it was time to go into the tunnel. When we ran out on to the field, the noise was incredible, something I had never experienced before.

Thankfully, Jimmy got himself into the game and by the second half, was feeling far more comfortable, as indeed were the shellshocked Blackpool side. They still lost 3-0 but had two golden opportunities towards the end and had a decent penalty appeal turned down. That was Jimmy's first-team debut for Blackpool FC.

The journey back was equally tiring. No time for a shower, so straight on to a bus at five o'clock before a train back to

London and the same hotel. The next morning, it was another bus to Euston, another train to Preston and a bus to Blackpool. Poor Jimmy would have loved to have stayed at home and rested but he almost immediately had to get a train to Lancaster to be back in his army barracks by teatime. On his return, his footballing moment of history was effectively ignored by his disinterested officers. Such was the life of a footballer in 1954. You could tell that story to the kids of today and they would never believe you. Oh, how things have changed.

By the way, Jimmy made his second appearance in the first team the following Saturday. It was at Old Trafford in a 4-1 defeat to Manchester United and, despite personal praise from manager Smith (something which was hard to come by), he was dropped back into the reserves and didn't play for the senior squad for the rest of the season. Breaking into the Blackpool side, even when they were struggling, was not an easy task. After seeing his colleagues and himself concede seven goals in two games, Jimmy may have felt it was better to keep away for a while anyway.

The army had to dominate his life now, especially as getting back to Blackpool from his new posting in Aldershot was not a thing of the moment. The already-mentioned lack of motorways, constant rail strikes and the demands of army life meant that he was away from home for long periods of time. It also meant he was away from the love of his life, Anne. They had begun dating some years before and it was clear the two of them were meant for each other, but army life was difficult for both of them. She would sometimes visit him, bringing sandwiches and cakes to beef up the scrawny man he had become under the harsh climate of National Service. It is a testament to both that the relationship not only survived the deprivations of that time but continued right up until Jimmy's death. 'Behind every great man is a stronger woman,' is a very familiar saying. It was probably born from Jimmy and Anne.

He carried on his training and eventually became a full-time PTI, putting new recruits through their paces, his life now a daily routine of 5am alarm calls, breakfast and being on parade two hours later. It was exhausting but it made more of the man that Jimmy became than if he'd never experienced such a life. Thankfully, by the time the new football season had arrived in August 1955, Jimmy had left Aldershot and was now able to play for the reserve team at Blackpool. It was an incredible schedule, one which almost defies belief today. On Thursdays, he would get a call from the club to see if he was available at the weekend (something which surely must prove how valuable he had become to Blackpool FC) and then, depending on where he was stationed, either Aldershot or later back in Lancaster, he would make his plans to return for a home game – or, if it was away, then make *major* plans to attend. There is a story he told of regularly being on guard duty through a Friday evening until 8am, picking up his boots, catching a bus to Blackpool, lying down to rest for an hour and then playing a full 90-minute game. Then, of course, there was the return journey afterwards. This was the love of football that this man had.

Call-up number three for the first team came in September 1955 for another away game, this time in front of 63,000 at Maine Road against Manchester City. It came about because of a long-term injury to regular Eddie Shimwell. Despite a good performance from the team and Jimmy, it was another loss, this time 2-0. In fact, Jimmy's first win was a week later on 1 October, with a 2-1 victory over Cardiff City. It was his first home game and a healthy crowd of 33,451 saw Jimmy start alongside George Farm, Hughie Kelly, Bill Perry, Stan Mortensen and Jackie Mudie. That attendance was actually around 4,500 down on the previous home game, against Wolverhampton Wanderers, when 38,098 turned up to see a 2-1 win. That figure remains to this day as the highest-ever attendance at Bloomfield Road for a Blackpool game. In what has become a regular tale of missing the great moments, Jimmy wasn't available to play in that game.

He did go on to play 31 times for the club that season, including an FA Cup defeat at Manchester City, and this was the season that Blackpool finished second in the First Division, their highest-ever position. They did, admittedly, finish 12 points behind champions Manchester United (when it was two points for a win) and they were never really close enough to be regarded as serious title contenders. There were some highlights, though. A 5-0 win over Charlton Athletic at home, 6-0 against Aston Villa and a 5-1 over Newcastle United, but a 6-2 home defeat to Preston North End (where George Farm, injured in goal, came back as an outfield player and actually scored Blackpool's opening goal) showed the frustrating inconsistency at the time.

Whilst turning out for Blackpool, Jimmy was also playing for numerous army teams all over the country. He would sometimes play three games a week, which doesn't seem too taxing – until you remember the travelling arrangements that came along with the schedule. There were numerous moments when he even had to hitch a ride back to Lancaster because he'd either missed the last bus or train or didn't have the money! A pound a week didn't go that far, even back in 1955. He was making a name for himself, though, being listed as one of the top 20 England prospects by the *Daily Express*.

In the mid-1950s, football in England (and Scotland, too) was the preserve of the working-class man. Grainy black-and-white photographs and film footage show thousands of flat-capped men stood shoulder to shoulder on the terraces, all swaying in unison with the motion of the crowd. No one wore colours and no one sang songs of a tribal nature. It was civilised and it was the game that everyone could play and participate in. Even those who played professionally, such as Jimmy, were not regarded as anything more special than the man who drove the bus to the stadium, with the supporters and players mingling together. Jimmy actually did walk to the stadium on matchdays, enjoying the banter between the supporters and players. This was the game that attracted him and the reason this is mentioned is that his love of football shines through his history. The 'best prospects' list was not one that suggested that a player would make the highest level and would one day own two mansions, three supercars and a private plane, but that they would have the honour of representing their country. That was reward enough.

By September 1956, Jimmy was demobbed, but even that wasn't without its trauma and doubt. It was at the time of the Suez Canal crisis and all National Service men and women were put on alert. If the invasion of Egypt by Britain, France and Israel was to result in an all-out war, then they were all to report back immediately to help the cause. Thankfully, no such war took place and Jimmy was able to forget the politics of a faraway place and continue his love affair with football. The Suez crisis proved that, even though the Second World War had finished over a decade previously, there were still enough hotspots in the world for National Service to be needed in the United Kingdom.

Britain in the 1950s was a far different place than today. At the beginning of the decade, cities were still scarred by bombed-out craters and unsafe and abandoned buildings. Rationing was an everyday chore for the housewife to deal with, as she queued for hours with her book in her hand for the latest piece of meat or fish that had made its way to the market. Three meals a day was a wish and a desire, as opposed to a certainty. Poverty pervaded most areas and a night out at the cinema (or 'pictures') was something to be looked forward to for weeks. There were promises of rebuilding the country but, by 1956, they were still promises.

The Suez crisis effectively brought to an end Great Britain's superpower standing in the world. Many countries of the Empire sought independence and, so, the Commonwealth was born. Immigration became a huge talking point, as shown in the Notting Hill riots of 1958, and the face of the country was changing on an almost daily basis. Youngsters had discovered rock 'n' roll and danced the night away in clubs in what, today, would seem like an innocent fashion but, in the 1950s, was perceived to be a corruption of the innocence of youth. By the time 1957 arrived, though, things had started to improve, with huge council flat buildings and tenement blocks rising above the bricks and bulldozers of the slums and grimy streets. Ironically, those buildings and tenement blocks played a part a decade later in the destruction of community life, something that Jimmy regarded as very important in his later life.

All of this was being played out in a Britain that was on its knees after winning the war. However, if there was one place that was unaffected, it was the entertainment capital of the country, Blackpool. Thousands flocked there daily, by train, by car, by coach and, still, by charabanc. The seven miles of golden sands, the tower, the pleasure beach, the donkey rides, the candy floss and 'tea to take away' were a paradise to those who lived in the sooty and grime-filled streets of Manchester and Liverpool. If there was ever a fine decision made, then the one made by Jimmy's mother at the start of the Second World War to relocate to Blackpool must have been one of the finest.

So, it was back to 'civvy street' and back to the aim of staying a professional footballer for James Christopher Armfield. Whereas many of his army colleagues left for an uncertain future, Jimmy went straight back to Blackpool and continued his football. There was another conversation with his father, who warned him of the pitfalls of being a footballer with a low wage and few prospects, but it was Jimmy's dream and no one was likely to get in the way of that.

Chapter Four:

Making his name ...

JIMMY WAS becoming established as a right-back for Blackpool, his name nearly always on a teamsheet that manager Joe Smith was reluctant to change unless absolutely necessary. The team was established in the First Division but its heyday was clearly in the past. Still, it had the most famous name in football wearing the tangerine shirt and showing little sign of wanting to slow down. Stanley Matthews, arguably one of the greatest footballers to come from these shores, was still bringing in record attendances all over the country. It became legend that when Stan played, there would be an extra 10,000 on the gate at the opposing ground, one of those myths that grows through the years until it becomes true, but it *was* true. A look at statistical guides to football seasons in the 1950s will show that if Everton were averaging 50,000 for their home matches, there would be at least 60,000 when Blackpool arrived with Stanley Matthews. It was the same throughout the land and one can only imagine the despair of those very same supporters who turned up in the cold and grey winter days to see 'The Maestro', only to find an annoying injury had kept him off the teamsheet that was rarely made public until 30 minutes before kick-off.

At first, Jimmy was completely in awe of the man he'd watched as a teenager and was now sharing a dressing room with. It's hardly surprising. Imagine having a hero, sporting or otherwise, and watching them from afar, then suddenly finding yourself doing the same things as him or her, but sadly not quite to the same level. Soon, though, Jimmy built up a rapport with the man who was twice his age and who basically dominated the Blackpool team so much that Joe Smith used to seriously say, 'If in doubt, give it to Stan.' This was the Stan who had an FA Cup Final named after him, despite team-mate Mortensen scoring the only hat-trick ever scored in the tournament's showpiece final. The Stan who played at a professional level for 33 years, whose England career spanned 23 years, who won the first European Player of the Year award, who was the first player to be knighted ... the list is almost endless. Imagine then, the forwardness and confidence of our Jimmy when, at the age of 22, he came up with a footballing proposal that was initially dismissed by Stan but eventually paved the way for one of the most radical departures for the role of defender and right-back. He suggested he became an overlapping full-back.

The idea was simple, but it's far easier to understand when you read Jimmy's words:

> I had been pondering a possible venture across the halfway line for some time before it actually happened. In just about every game, the opposition double marked Stanley, with their left-winger dropping back to make

the first tackle and the left-back waiting behind him should Matthews get past. This left me in acres of open space. So, one day, I had a quiet word with Stan and told him my plan. I would sprint around his two markers on the outside and when I was in the clear, Stan could slip the ball into the open space ahead of me. He declined to comment and the idea went on to the backburner.

It didn't, though, because in the home game with Luton Town at the start of the 1957/58 season, they tried it and it worked! Well, it worked to the point that Jimmy suddenly found himself clear on the right of goal with no one near him. Unfortunately, the perfect script he had written in his mind wasn't followed. He fluffed his lines and shot well wide, something which didn't impress manager Smith. His comment that Blackpool 'didn't need another number seven, because the one they've got was doing a pretty good job' was crushing enough for it not to be tried for another couple of months. When it was, against Wolves, it worked perfectly and suddenly the 'overlapping full-back' was born. Jimmy Armfield was the first, with a little help from the greatest footballer of his generation.

There's no doubt that Stan was a difficult man to impress. Not exactly a loner in the dressing room, he did do things in his own way. His training methods were different and separate from the squad, his dietary regime was so far advanced that physical preparation experts would even today question the wisdom of it, and he knew he was the best. It wasn't arrogance, but he just knew. Jimmy again came across that individualistic behaviour when he came off the pitch after 90 gruelling minutes against Leicester City in September 1959. Gruelling because Blackpool had drawn 3-3 after being 3-0 down; and guess who got the equaliser late into the game?

When Jimmy first started playing football, he played as a striker, as most youngsters did. It was more fun, there was more glory and scoring goals is what makes football. He was actually quite good at it, as recorded earlier in the book, but his transition to full-back was easier and he developed the position better than virtually anyone else. Every now and then, though, that goalscoring itch needed a scratch and, in the game against Leicester, Jimmy gloried in putting the ball into the net and gaining a vital one point when it seemed the cause was lost.

'Why did you put your arm up as you came off the field?' This was the response of Stanley Matthews as they trudged into the dressing room. He didn't appear to be happy with the team's performance.

'Well, the crowd were cheering me,' was the genuinely surprised response, voice deflated and shoulders now sagging.

'Yes, because they knew you'd played well but you don't need to respond like that,' and that was it. That was Stanley Matthews' reaction to Jimmy Armfield scoring his first-ever professional goal for Blackpool Football Club.

It seems churlish today, in a time when a player does what he is paid for and rewards the adoring and ecstatic fans by running to the crowd, kissing the badge on his shirt, making a heart shape with his hands and cupping an ear to the away supporters in a 'look at what I've just done' moment, but to be fair to Matthews, he didn't behave that way, either. It was a lesson to Jimmy that it was the team that was important and not him. The Matthews of 'there were 11 on the pitch at Wembley' was genuine and this stayed with Jimmy for the rest of his career. Maybe this had a big part to play on the day that Jimmy sat in the stands at Wembley on England's greatest day? No histrionics, no petulant behaviour, just acceptance, because the team came first. As an aside, the problem with Jimmy celebrating a goal didn't really bother him too many times after that. He only scored five more times in his career, including a prolific 1964/65 season in which he scored twice!

Blackpool were now a spent force as potential winners of any type of competition and it was clear that the board had decided a change was needed. So, at the end of the 1957/58 season, they dismissed Joe Smith. It was an astonishing decision, as he had been Blackpool manager for 23 years and had transformed a lowly Second Division club into one of the powerhouses of English football, with three FA Cup Final appearances, including one Wembley victory in 1953, and a second-place finish in the First Division. Given this, his sacking was tawdry at best, with a telegram delivered to his home on the Saturday morning *after* the team had left for an away game at Aston Villa. It was the end of an incredible era, with many of the great players leaving for pastures new. Jimmy stayed, though, despite having been the subject of interest from Manchester United that season.

In the pre-Munich air disaster days, United had one of the best teams in the country and were quickly building their reputation as one of the world's largest and most popular clubs. Matt Busby was the manager of a team that included numerous stars and household names, Duncan Edwards being the one who is mentioned the most when recounting tales from that era. Busby had taken a liking to Jimmy after twice seeing him play for Blackpool against his team in September 1957. He immediately contacted Joe Smith, who gave no encouragement to the proposed deal, and Jimmy stayed. Not that he knew about the bid at the time. It was a few days later that Joe Smith broke the news to him, but in one of those odd moments that life could bring up, it meant that Jimmy's love affair with Blackpool continued and it also meant that Jimmy was never aboard the ill-fated flight from Munich in February 1958, something which he almost certainly would have been, bearing in mind he was now a regular first-team player.

Whatever you want to call it, it is one of those moments in life where you just wonder. If Joe Smith had informed him of the bid and if Jimmy had agreed to join Manchester United, then the potential different outcome is a chilling one. All ifs and buts, of course, but these are the moments of life.

Smith was replaced as manager by Ron Suart and a more different character one could not have found. He immediately set about rebuilding the team, bringing in new faces but also keeping the backbone of the team that had been so successful earlier in the decade. Jimmy was part of that and he found Suart a far more adventurous manager, without the easy-going nature of the jovial, but at times surly, Smith. In his first season in charge, Suart took Blackpool to a respectable eighth place in the league but that remains the last time the club finished in the top half of the top flight. A sad statistic for a club of whom one ex-player had once said in an interview: 'The First

Division without Blackpool is like strawberries without cream.' It was said a long time previous, but it was as relevant at that time as it had been before. The cream had now curdled and the strawberries had lost their flavour. Blackpool, with Jimmy, were having to face some very difficult times ahead.

By this time, Jimmy had started to make his mark at international level. It wasn't in the full England team, as that was another few years away, but in the Under-23 team. This was at a time when playing for the under-23s meant you were actually under 23 years of age! Jimmy was chosen to play at right-back for England against Scotland at Hillsborough at the age of just 20. Sadly, he had to withdraw due to tonsilitis and one can only imagine the despair and frustration he must have felt as the excitement of putting on the white England jersey for the first time was taken away from him. He'd heard about his call-up whilst still doing his National Service in Scotland and had travelled down to Sheffield with three others by train. Unfortunately, by the time he arrived, a high temperature and aching bones suggested there was something amiss and he was confined to bed at the hotel. Was there ever a more disappointing journey?

Thankfully, England manager Walter Winterbottom saw in Jimmy what most others had started to see, an incredibly fast and talented young player who was clearly destined to play at the highest level for his country. He'd already appeared for the Football League against the Irish League in Belfast and, despite a 5-2 thrashing, Jimmy had been given rave reviews in reports.

So, just five days after his 21st birthday, Jimmy Armfield made his first England Under-23 appearance in Copenhagen against Denmark. There were 25,000 spectators present (which goes to show how the passion for football was spreading all over the world) and it was the first game in Denmark under floodlights. That was a novelty in itself. It didn't help the Danes, though, who were presumably blinded by the artificial light in a land where the sun doesn't shine that brightly and they were soundly beaten 3-0.

Of as much interest, though, was the travel itinerary to and from the country. The squad (or team as it was more accurately described in those days), actually met up in London two days beforehand and caught a mid-morning flight from London Airport on the Tuesday, the day before the game. Their return was the following morning, an itinerary giving very little time for acclimatisation or rest or, indeed, any type of pre-match practice. Such were the ways of 1956. Sadly, there was little coverage of Jimmy in the newspaper reports the next day but that could easily have been explained by the fact that it was such a dominant victory (with a fourth goal effectively ruled out as the referee had blown the final whistle) that England's defenders weren't in great demand that evening. Anyway, unlike his club and Football League career, Jimmy kicked off his international career with a win. It also came with a nice and welcome match fee of £15 from the FA and, rather bizarrely, a bottle opener from the Danish Football Federation.

There then followed an England 'B' tour of three Balkan countries (a level where players turned out in an England shirt but didn't actually receive a cap) in which Jimmy played in all three matches. The first game, a 2-1 defeat against Bulgaria in front of 55,000 fans, was notable for an appalling tackle by

Sunderland's Stan Anderson that saw him sent off and having to be surrounded by security men and police to protect him as he left the pitch. Having said that, Jimmy's take on the tackle in his autobiography is completely different to the ones reported extensively by the newspapers the next day.

Bulgaria certainly left its mark on Jimmy and the whole team. There was a huge anti-Western feeling in the country, where communism was embraced emphatically. The hotel was of typical Soviet Bloc 'luxury', with two hard beds, a carpet covering a stone floor, a stained sink and an uncovered light bulb badly illuminating the 'grandeur'. Most managed to cope but a certain young player by the name of Brian Clough was beginning to find a voice to match his high footballing ability and expressed his disdain to just about anyone who couldn't avoid him. At least the nightly card games kept the boredom at bay. The food was so bad that one of the players, Jimmy Bloomfield, took on chef duties in the kitchen and kept the team sustained with soup and boiled eggs.

The second game was a 1-0 win against Romania in front of around 100,000 spectators and this was officially the first time an England side had won behind the Iron Curtain. The story of this game is that of the coach carrying the team to the stadium driving through deserted streets. There was no one around and no sign that a game of football was being played. It was only once the players trudged on to the uneven surface that they noticed the huge number of spectators just sitting there in polite silence. That changed come the game and the atmosphere was described as 'hostile' by the *Daily Mail* the next day. Their hotel was also where Polish and Danish female gymnasts, who were competing in the European Championships, were staying; a pleasant distraction for the England players. All in all, the England tourists found Romania to be a far more friendly and welcoming country than Bulgaria.

The final game was a comfortable Duncan Edwards-led 2-0 win against Czechoslovakia. It had been an exhausting tour with three games in 12 days and numerous flights, substandard hotels and little in the way of training and practice. This, of course, was taking place after the domestic season had just ended, with Blackpool finishing a creditable fourth. Jimmy returned to Under-23 action in October of that year in a 3-2 win over Romania at Wembley, the first time England had won at that level at the old Empire Stadium.

Certainly, 1958 was a year to remember for Jimmy. In June, he married Anne, the girl he had met when he was a child during the war and the girl he fell in love with when he was doing his National Service. They were the perfect couple. Anne was Jimmy's rock and stood by him throughout his career.

Later that year, Ron Greenwood, who had taken over the duties as England Under-23 manager, was so impressed with young Jimmy that he gave him the captaincy for the game at Hillsborough against Poland in front of 38,000 fans. It was an easy victory – 4-1 – with a hat-trick from Bobby Charlton on a night when monsoon-like rains hit the stadium. For Jimmy, it was a sign of things to come. At the age of 23, he was captaining his country at Under-23 level. That date – 24 October – was another date from 1958 that stayed in his memory for many years to come, marking a remarkable rise for the youngster who had only been a regular in the Blackpool side for a couple of years. A month later, he captained the Under-23s again, this time at Carrow Road as England beat Czechoslovakia 3-0, and, with the selectors due to meet the next day, there was a suggestion he might be chosen for a full international cap in the upcoming fixture with the Soviet Union at Wembley, but that step was one that they, and he, were not quite ready to take. It would come soon, however.

It was a year that saw Jimmy Armfield rise to prominence in the footballing world and the year that saw him marry his childhood sweetheart, if that isn't too much of a cliché. Blackpool Football Club had given him a terraced house (with rent to be paid, of course) and had bought his first car, a black Morris Minor, which sat proudly in the driveway. There is a story that he tells in his autobiography of building a garage to house the vehicle, but the club (ever mindful of money, of course) ordered him to either pay extra rent or tear it down. He chose to pay the rent, baffled by the directors' inability to see that the garage had actually added value to the property. Some things tend not to change and many directors at the club before and since have looked at life in exactly the same way!

Chapter Five:

England calls ...

IN MARCH 1959, Jimmy played in an England Under-23 game against France in Lyon. It was a drab 1-1 draw in front of a crowd of 12,000 totally disinterested spectators, most of whom had little idea a game of football was being played that afternoon, as there had been virtually no publicity leading up to the match. It was different two months later in Milan against Italy in what was a defining moment in Jimmy's career.

Italy had never beaten England at any level at that point. The day before, the senior teams had drawn 2-2 at Wembley and, buoyed by that result, around 80,000 fans packed into the stadium in the hope that, at long last, some Italian history was about to be made. The opening of the *Daily Mirror* report the next day, explains what happened:

> For the first time in years an English soccer team was cheered long, loud and gloriously by foreign fans after those [sic] heart-swelling victory here today. At the end, armed police had to rescue the Italian team from their own crowd as fans hooted and shouted 'dustbins'

at them. But for Young England it was applause all the way. They did not just beat Italy, they showed them how the game should be played. The Italian supporters were cascading cushions on the pitch in disgust long before the end.

For the record, England won 3-0 and it was a celebratory evening that followed for the England players, except for three men – Walter Winterbottom, Jimmy Greaves and Jimmy Armfield. The reason? They were leaving the Under-23 tour party, who were off to West Germany the next day, and Winterbottom and his two youngsters were catching an overnight train to Zürich, where they would be meeting up with the full international England squad for a flight to Rio and Brazil. It was crazy.

At this point, Jimmy, at the age of 23, had played at the top level for his hometown team Blackpool, captained England at Under-23 level and was now on his way to the other side of the world to make his debut for his national side. It must have been overwhelming, if not incredibly exciting. Even today, in this age of travel and a much smaller world, being told to catch a flight to Brazil the next morning, when you had been expecting to be travelling to West Germany, would be a moment to remember. For Jimmy, this was his footballing coming of age.

There was just enough time to call home and explain to Anne, his loyal and trustworthy wife, plus his mother and father, and then it was the long and tedious flight to Rio. Tedious because of fuel stops, but that was dampened by the enthusiasm Jimmy must have had for what was ahead.

Rio was like a different world to Blackpool. There was the sea and there was a beach, but that was where the similarities ended. The heat was oppressive and everywhere the team looked there were children playing football, either on the beach or in the streets. Brazil were the new world champions and they boasted Julinho, Didi and, of course, Pelé, arguably the greatest footballer of all time. There was a feeling in the country that Brazil had an almost divine right to win and that, at that point in time, there were few teams who could match them.

Jimmy was actually asked to play at left-back, a position he didn't know that well, to try and stem the forward attacks from Julinho and Didi, with Don Howe playing at right-back. It's fair to say the game at the Maracanã Stadium left its mark on him in many ways. There is a photograph that, even though in black and white, illustrates the obvious fervour and colour of the Brazilian fans in the background. Jimmy, in his gleaming white shirt with, for him, the unfamiliar number three on his back, is stood there facing the camera. He has his arms folded and is smiling. For all the world to see, he was proud and he was excited. He was making his England debut and he was playing against the world champions in one of the biggest stadiums in the world. No matter how much he downplayed it afterwards (and it's interesting to see how little he refers to it in his autobiography), it was an incredible moment for the young man.

The kick-off was delayed, as we have already heard, and within 90 seconds, Jimmy touched the ball – but only to pick it out of the net. In an almost carbon copy repeat of his Blackpool debut, the game seemed to have started without him (or any of the rest of the team to be fair). Julinho had scored and within another 25 minutes it was 2-0. Brazil were rampant and England were barely hanging on.

Take a moment to reflect on this. The England team, which included Billy Wright, Johnny Haynes and Bobby Charlton, were effectively sheep being thrown to the wolves, with a feverish crowd of around 160,000 fans baying for blood (in the nicest possible sense. Brazilian fans are fair, but also passionate). Jimmy was making his debut and, within 90 seconds, the man he'd been asked to mark had already scored and Jimmy hadn't touched the ball. The strength of self-discipline and self-belief must have been very strong at that point and, to be fair to Jimmy, he and the team played far better in the second half – apparently helped by a sniff of oxygen from a canister to overcome the unfamiliar heat, humidity and altitude. It was a sobering moment for a team that genuinely believed it had a chance of winning the next World Cup in 1962. They weren't even on the same playing field at times. This is how it was described in the *Football Yearbook* of 1959:

> England's first match of a four-game summer tour was a minor test against the new world champions in front of 185,000 screaming fans in the Maracanã Stadium in Rio. Bobby Charlton and Johnny Haynes rapped shots against the post after England had gone 2-0 down to early goals against a Brazilian team that featured both Didi and Pelé in a rare appearance together. Blackpool's Jimmy Armfield was given a chasing he will not forget by Julinho, in what was a baptism of fire for the Blackpool defender. He was

called in to partner Don Howe in an out-of-club position at left-back. Norman Deeley, small, direct Wolves winger, was the fifth player to wear the number seven shirt since the departure of the one and only Tom Finney. Goalkeeper Eddie Hopkinson saved two certain goals from Pelé but could do nothing to stop a thunderbolt from Julinho, who had been picked in preference to the great Garrincha. As Eddie Hopkinson lay on the ground after being beaten all ends up by Julinho's shot, a posse of Brazilian radio commentators rushed on to the pitch to try to interview him. It is just as well that they could not translate his direct comments delivered in Lancastrian tones! England were well and truly beaten by the world champions and did well to keep their score down to just two goals. Didi and Pelé together was just about the most potent combination that any team in the world could put together. Ronnie Clayton clattered into Pelé with a tackle that led to 'The King' being carried off on a stretcher for treatment. He soon came back, but for the rest of the game Clayton's life was made hell by the Brazilians fans who would not forgive him for hurting their idol. Shortly before he was carried off, Pelé missed a sitter right in front of an open goal. He was human, after all.

As a thank you for their participation, the Brazilian Football Association presented each England player with a certificate showing that they now owned a small piece of the Amazon rainforest. Whether any of these little patches of the earth's lungs are still standing is, sadly, not known. There was also an aquamarine stone presented to each player and member of the backroom staff. Jimmy's was eventually made into a ring for Anne but, sadly, it was lost when the Armfield house was burgled some years later. That sentence is simplistic in its description but it must hide the pain and despair of the moment.

Four days later, England were thrashed by Peru 4-1 in what was described as a 'lacklustre performance', Chelsea's Jimmy Greaves scoring the only goal for England. That was followed a week later by a 2-1 defeat in Mexico, complete with 100-degree Fahrenheit heat and serious breathing difficulties for most of the team due to the altitude. The game was notable for two events from an England point of view. The first was that two substitutes were used in the same match for the first time by an England international team and the second being that Blackburn's Ronnie Clayton was seriously sunburnt and had to have medical treatment from the Mexican team doctor both during and after the match. England hadn't brought their own doctor on tour, something which was to change in the immediate future.

The final match of this quite disastrous tour was in Los Angeles against the United States. The baseball ground of Wrigley Field played host to around 13,000 confused spectators who seemed to know nothing of soccer and saw England romp to an 8-1 victory after being a goal down and then seeing the US have another one disallowed. It saved any embarrassment such as the still remembered and talked about 1950 1-0 defeat in the World Cup, but the game was notable in England's minds for the fact that it was Billy Wright's 105th and final game for his country. It was an international career that started in Belfast in

1946 and finished in Los Angeles when Wright captained his country for the 90th time.

It had been an arduous tour and, for the young Jimmy Armfield, a moment of reckoning. His first taste of senior international football had come after he had initially been expecting to be playing for the Under-23s and he had acquitted himself well in a team that had some major star players, even though he had been played out of position in all four games. Playing at left-back wasn't a problem but it didn't come naturally to him and the 'baptism of fire', as it was described against Brazil, really showed where he was at his best – and that wasn't on the left of the field. Speaking to Walter Winterbottom on the flight back to the UK, it was clear they both shared the same view and the England manager promised to give it some thought (and great credit to the young Jimmy for suggesting it to the experienced Winterbottom). Jimmy would never play at left-back for his country again.

Although Jimmy was still playing for a now sinking Blackpool, who spent most of the 1959/60 season in mid-table, he was being noticed around the country. It's incredible to think that if he was playing today there would have been constant rumours of a 'big club' move, but this was a matter of months before the players' maximum wage was abolished, so there was little incentive on either side. Still, his peers recognised his worth and, after returning from the tour with England, he was voted as the very first 'Young Footballer of the Year', a prize sponsored by the *News Chronicle*.

It was a great honour to be nominated as the first recipient, but unfortunately the award wasn't something that survived too long. Jimmy Greaves won it the following year and then it quietly faded away. At least Jimmy Armfield received a silver cap, plus a silver football from Blackpool Corporation and had the pleasure of receiving both awards in the ballroom at the tower, presented by Billy Wright and his wife, Joy, part of the incredibly popular Beverley Sisters.

At this time, England were building up towards the 1962 World Cup and Jimmy was now an integral part of those plans. The British Championship (or Home Championship as they were to become known) was an important preparation, spread across the season from October until April. England's first two games in the 1959/60 championship, against Wales and Northern Ireland, didn't see Jimmy appear. Don Howe had kept his right-back position and, after Jimmy made his feelings known about playing at left-back, he was replaced by Tony Allen of Stoke. Whatever the reasons, England didn't fare well, drawing 1-1 with Wales and scrambling to a 2-1 win over the Northern Irish at Wembley. The title decider was at Hampden Park against Scotland on 9 April 1960. Jimmy was back and playing in his preferred right-back position with Ray Wilson of Huddersfield at left-back (Wilson actually ended up playing the game with a broken nose after an early collision).

Anyone who visited the old Hampden Park before it was modernised (and sanitised, it seems), will recall the intensity of passion and the sheer overwhelming noise made by the Scottish fans. Even in those days, the stadium was segregated, with Celtic and Rangers supporters kept apart, both with a mutual loathing of each other but both there for a common purpose – to see Scotland beat the 'Auld Enemy'.

Actually, Scotland hadn't beaten England at home since 1937, so expectation was high, especially as England's form was patchy, to say the least. Just under 130,000 fans crammed into the ground on a cold spring day, with virtually no English support at a time when travelling from England to Scotland wasn't the easiest of endeavours. Scotland should have won, as they dominated the game, but it was a scrappy affair, not helped by a referee who awarded 55 free kicks and two penalties. Bobby Charlton had scored from the penalty spot to equalise just after half-time. It ended 1-1, with Charlton wasting a second penalty towards the end – seeing his first effort saved and then missing the target when the referee ordered a retake – to give the Scots a huge let-off.

Jimmy said that the game was a real stride forward in his international career, although there are few, if any, mentions of him in the newspaper reports that followed. It was good enough that he had played in such an intense atmosphere and had not put a foot wrong but then Jimmy rarely did. As a matter of interest, the championship was shared by England, Scotland and Wales, who all finished tied, whilst Northern Ireland failed to pick up a single point.

The international season extended to the end of May and Jimmy played in all three of the remaining games. There was a 3-3 home draw with Yugoslavia, courtesy of a last-minute equaliser by Johnny Haynes, a 3-0 defeat in Spain, where Jimmy was named as England's man of the match for the way he man-marked Real Madrid's Francisco Gento, and a 2-0 defeat away to Hungary. The results didn't look good but manager Walter Winterbottom and the rest of the FA selection committee had seen enough to encourage them. In the summer, Winterbottom gathered his players at Lilleshall and told them that, barring injuries, they would make up the squad to prepare for the World Cup. Jimmy was part of that group. He'd played eight times for England and, after returning against Scotland, he played 37 of the next 38 games for his country at right-back. His England career was settled.

Chapter Six:

Blackpool crisis and the maximum wage

WHILST HIS England career was taking off, Jimmy's club career with Blackpool had stalled. Not stalled in the way he was playing but in the way the team, now bereft of its major stars, were sliding inexorably down the league pyramid. In the 1960/61 season, they only won one of their first 15 league and cup games, sitting firmly at the bottom of the First Division. By the end of the season, they'd climbed to 20th, avoiding relegation by just one point, gained in the final match of the season in a 3-3 draw with Manchester City. Although the club retained its top-flight status for another six seasons, its best days were behind it. Jimmy played in a team that was losing as many as it won and in front of a Bloomfield Road crowd that was diminishing in numbers season on season.

Of course, this was the footballing era of the maximum wage. Players in those days weren't looked upon as natural assets to the clubs they played for. They were seen as employees and little else. The romantic idea of the players walking to the ground with the spectators was true but the men who would then entertain those spectators were very rarely paid any more than them and, in some cases, even less. They were regarded, to a certain extent, as unintelligent people who did not have a true career skill and had few prospects outside the game.

Transfer fees were normally respectable and a player, if he had looked after himself, could retire to a trade that he had learned whilst playing the game, although most seemed to fall back on shop-owning or, perhaps inevitably, running a public house. Jimmy, for instance, took up the far higher-level career of journalism, but that's a tale we will revisit later in the book. Footballers never became rich. They became famous, in a very stunted 1950s–60s way, but never wealthy. The factory owners, the committees, the born-to-privilege were the ones who made, and kept, money in the game. The players were just there to put on a show. Then it all changed.

There had been a football union in the past. As early as 1907, a Players' Union was set up by Manchester City's Billy Meredith. This came about due to an incident involving one of his team-mates five years earlier. DJ Jones had cut his knee on some broken glass in a pre-season friendly. The wound became infected and poor DJ died, leaving behind a wife and child. Manchester City refused to pay any compensation, arguing that the game was a friendly and, therefore, Jones was not 'working', which seems just about the harshest possible response imaginable.

At that time, a player could earn £4 a week, reducing to £3 in the summer, and even by 1953 and the 'Matthews Final', it was £15 and £13, respectively. So, it was hardly surprising that a gift of a cigarette lighter to each member of the Wembley-winning team that season was seen as extravagant.

It all changed in 1961. Jimmy Hill, future football pundit but at this time a regular Coventry City player, managed to persuade the Professional Footballers' Association (PFA) to call for a strike unless the maximum wage of £20 per week was abolished. This rather annoyed the Pools companies, which made a lot of money every weekend, and the club owners. The thought of a football strike seemed impossible to them and they certainly wouldn't accept the thought of weekends without football. A few backed Hill's stance, though, most notably Burnley chairman Bob Lord, whereas the Blackburn Rovers chairman, Jim Wilkinson, announced that it would be a suicide pact for all football clubs. The strike was called for 21 January.

The public support was huge, with calls for boycotts of games (proving that the modern-day Blackpool supporter boycott against their owners was not as unique as believed, even if it was hugely successful). With 72 hours to go, the Football League backed down and the maximum wage was abolished. That wasn't the end of the story, though. The strike was set to continue, as there had been no mention of the archaic 'retain and transfer' system. This basically enabled a club to retain the services of a player beyond his contract if he didn't want to stay and pay him less for the privilege!

It was George Eastham who took the League to court and continued proceedings after his club, Newcastle United, finally agreed to sell him to Arsenal. Eventually, the strike was called off and Hill's Fulham team-mate, Johnny Haynes, was the first to really benefit, becoming the country's first £100-per-week footballer.

The meeting that decided the outcome was held at Belle Vue in Manchester. Hill was chairing it, with a large gathering of players in the hall, some for and some against. Stanley Matthews was present and it's fair to say that he was the man they were all looking to for guidance. Jimmy recounted the tale many times in his life and regularly told the story in his regular after dinner speeches.

A young player from the lower divisions stood up and gave the audience his view. 'My dad's a miner', he said, 'earning £10 a week … I play in the lower divisions and I earn twice as much. I train in the open air and I play on a Saturday … he's down the pit for eight hours at a time, five days a week. That can't be right.'

'I'll answer that Mr Chairman …' and I looked around to see that it was the Bolton Wanderers left-back Tommy Banks. 'Now then son, thee tell thi father from me,' in his broad Lancashire accent, 'I can do his job. In fact, I have and so can any of these lads in this hall, including thee, but if thi father wants to know why we want more brass, tell him to come and play our Stan in front of 30,000 fans. That's why we want more money.'

I remember the room in the Belle Vue Hall erupting in laughter and cheers. No one laughed or cheered more than Stanley Matthews and I believe that was the moment everyone agreed … I had been on £20 a week before the strike and my pay doubled to £40. I thought I was a millionaire!

Different times. Jimmy actually went to see the board shortly afterwards when he heard about Haynes and his £100 weekly wage but they didn't relent, only offering an extra £5 a week. However, the abolition of the maximum wage was a victory for the players and it was a turning point in the game of football in England. For Jimmy, it didn't make him rich, though. Even in 1970, he was still earning just £75 per week plus appearance money and bonuses. It wasn't a bad wage for the time but it wasn't a rich wage. Again, different times.

The problem with the abolition of the maximum wage from a club like Blackpool's point of view was that it basically spelled the end of any hope of competing at the top. Blackpool have never been a big club and, even in their heyday, when they regularly challenged for the title and made numerous Wembley appearances, they couldn't average more than 25,000 regular supporters. Compare that to the likes of Everton and Manchester United, who would attract crowds of 60,000 to 70,000 every other weekend, and therein lies the problem.

In the 1960s, football clubs didn't make money. They didn't exist to take the change out of a spectator's pocket with temptations of a new replica shirt or the latest pair of boots. They didn't lose too much either if they were competitive but the only source of income was matchday, where gate receipts and programme sales brought in the money. It wasn't lost on many that Blackpool climbed out of debt during the Second World War after the military rented Bloomfield Road for storage space. When Blackburn Rovers' Jim Wilkinson made his comment about it being footballing suicide if the maximum wage was abolished, you could see that he had a point. Clubs of that size could now only watch helplessly as their best players were tempted by larger rewards at bigger clubs and, in turn, those clubs and their signings enjoyed more success.

Despite all this, Jimmy stayed at Blackpool. He was one of the rising stars of English football and was attracting attention but the club never released any information as to whether he was wanted by others. That presumably meant that Jimmy was kept in the dark, too. A restriction of trade? Having said that, it was clear when I knew him and it was clear in those much earlier days, too, that Jimmy's heart was always in Blackpool. The Armfields' first child, Duncan, was born in November 1961, followed by John in March 1963, and Jimmy supplied a stable and loving life for his family. He actually didn't want to leave Blackpool. He was loyal to the town and he certainly didn't want to uproot his family to chase footballing glory elsewhere. Even many years later, when he had been appointed Leeds United manager, he kept his family in Blackpool, preferring to commute and stay in temporary accommodation. As Duncan said:

> He didn't want to uproot us, even then when me and John were in our early teens and at school. He wanted a stable family life for us all and I know my mother was happy to stay in Blackpool … so it was never an issue.

Jimmy was asked many times in his later years as to why he never left Blackpool – a wonderful club but one that was struggling to keep up with the fast-moving chase for success. It was simple as far as he was concerned, as he explained in this quote from the 1971 book *Blackpool Football* by Robin Daniels:

> Some chaps move from club to club, they're just out to make a fast buck. They can't have many real friends. They must have missed a lot along the way and I feel very sorry for them. They probably make far more money than I'll ever make in football. It all depends on where you pitch your ambition. Is it how well or how long you play? Is it all the pleasure you get from playing? Or is it the money?

Jimmy stayed with Blackpool, who continued their slow slide downwards, whilst England seemed to be on the verge of something quite spectacular under Walter Winterbottom. Jimmy's footballing ambitions now seemed to be totally linked to England and especially the upcoming 1962 World Cup.

Chapter Seven:

1962 World Cup

THE BUILD-UP to the World Cup finals really began in 1960 – on 8 October to be exact. Whilst Blackpool were being beaten 5-2 at home by Fulham, and so cementing their bottom position in The First Division, Jimmy was playing for England in the opening Home Championship game away to Northern Ireland and winning by the same scoreline. It was the first of a remarkable run of victories under the newly rejuvenated England team, which, over the next six months, won seven of their next nine games, scoring 45 goals in the process. This included a 9-0 World Cup qualifying victory over Luxembourg, an 8-0 Wembley friendly win against Mexico and a 9-3 hammering of Scotland at Wembley to win the Home International Championship with maximum points.

A 4-2 home friendly victory over Spain at Wembley saw Jimmy praised in match reports for the way he handled the world-class winger Francisco Gento, a player he had encountered in Madrid the previous year, but in a World Cup qualifier later in the year, at Highbury against Luxembourg, he was not spared the boos and jeers as the team struggled to a 4-2 victory over the part-timers. Football fans are nothing if not fickle. A few weeks later, he played against Wales at Cardiff with a torn muscle and was applauded off the pitch by appreciative Welsh fans after a 1-1 draw. Sometimes, you just can't win.

England booked their qualification for the World Cup finals with a 2-0 Wembley victory over Portugal on 25 October 1961. Jimmy won his 20th cap and the gate receipts were a record £52,000 from the 100,000 crowd. Those are the statistics but the excitement and relief from that day was palpable. England were becoming a force in international football and they approached the finals in confident mood. It didn't seem to be transmitting itself to the ever-critical supporters, though, as one month later a new record low crowd of just 30,000 turned up at Wembley to see a turgid 1-1 draw with Northern Ireland in the Home Championship.

Sadly, just as the confidence soared, the results plummeted. For the first time in history, England failed to win a game in the Home Championship, which culminated in a dominant 2-0 Scotland win at Hampden Park in front of 132,000. It didn't faze Jimmy, though, and he later said that the England team at that time was the best he'd ever played in. The team were ready for Chile and all that the World Cup could throw at them, even if the reaction from the English supporters and media was lukewarm at best. Their last game before setting off for South America was a friendly against Switzerland at Wembley. Only 35,000 bothered to make the journey on a dark and windy Wednesday afternoon. Next stop, Chile! The contrast could not have been starker.

The squad set of for Chile in May 1962 and, as Jimmy said in his autobiography, it was a journey that seemed to be never-ending. There were numerous stops on the way from London to Lima in Peru and it was an exhausted party that arrived at their first destination. They were buoyant, though, as there was a definite inner belief that this group of players were capable of winning the World Cup, even if the press and fans didn't see it the same way. As is always the case in these moments, the players and the rest aren't always aligned. How many times in recent years has the cry gone up from fans and the press to say that England were on the verge of glory when the players themselves did not truly believe it? In 1962, though, it was the other way round. It was the players who believed that a trophy was imminent, even if the few press members, and even fewer spectators who followed them across the world, had little appetite for such bravado.

England were in Peru for a warm-up game in Lima. A sweltering afternoon, a small but partisan crowd and a 4-0 victory, courtesy of a Jimmy Greaves hat-trick, suggested that their confidence was well placed. It was also the game that saw a certain Bobby Moore make his debut in place of the injured Bobby Robson. There is an amusing story told of the celebration meal that evening, when both Jimmy and Bobby Charlton had been invited to sing on stage at a restaurant, where they thought they hadn't been recognised. There was no chance of refusing, as the other diners were clearly star-struck, and so the two sang a pretty decent rendition of 'Mr Sandman', only to see Walter Winterbottom watching from the far side of the room. He wasn't impressed but decided that it was good for international relations! The next morning, the squad set off on their final leg of the journey to Chile.

Today, the World Cup is the biggest footballing tournament in the world – arguably the biggest sporting tournament, too – but in 1962, it was a rather underplayed affair. Although there was tremendous interest around the globe, and especially for the 16 nations competing, the actual hosting of the event was completely different from anything likely to be seen today. Two years previously, there had been a massive earthquake in Chile and this had put an enormous amount of pressure on a country that had never hosted such an event before and few people in Chile had confidence in their ability to pull it off. Chile persevered, though, determined to show the doubters that their little-known and earthquake-ravaged country could deliver on its promises. Due to the effects of the earthquake, the organisers had to make major changes to the venues, some being discarded, whilst others attempted to be rebuilt in time.

Eventually, only four stadiums were used, three of them with an average capacity of around 18,000, with the main stadium in the capital city Santiago holding 66,000. The England squad found themselves based in a town called Coya on a site that belonged to the Staff House Braden Copper Company. This was so far away from just about anything that the sight of tumbleweed rolling across a breezy dust-laden road would not have surprised anyone. How on earth the England backroom staff even found the place is a mystery in itself, but find it they did, even if the players weren't exactly appreciative.

As Jimmy mentions in his book, it was a nightmare journey to even get to their base, which was effectively a near-deserted town, 8,000ft above sea level and a 90-minute journey from Santiago. To travel there, they had to take a bus and then a one-carriage train up the mountain, with spectacular views and llamas to keep them company, before arriving at a selection of small bungalows that would house the players and staff. There was little in the way of entertainment, apart from a cinema – that showed films of interest only to those who spoke Spanish – and a nine-hole golf course. When the opening ceremony took place, they all had to catch the same train and bus to Rancagua, where the three other squads in England's group – Hungary, Argentina and Bulgaria – stood alongside the English players in the main square and listened to badly played national anthems. The squads of the other 12 nations had their own opening ceremonies in similar style. Then it was back again for the England players. It was certainly a challenge. A different time.

The tournament was not regarded as a success, as there were numerous violent incidents on the pitch between the players, most notably the game between hosts Chile and Italy. This became known as 'the Battle of Santiago', which is a little unimaginative, and came about after an Italian journalist wrote of the capital city: 'It is a proudly backwards and a poverty-stricken dump full of prostitution and crime.'

Obviously, that didn't go down well, but thankfully England weren't involved in such things. They were here to win the World Cup! It didn't get off to the best start, though. In front of a crowd of just 7,900, they lost 2-1 to Hungary through a late winner. The newspapers hardly mentioned Jimmy in their reports but they were scathing about the team in general. The weather had been wet and a mistake by Ron Flowers to gift the Hungarians victory was not excused. The team returned to their 'luxury' accommodation feeling depressed and frustrated.

Whatever expectations they had of this particular period in their playing careers, they were rapidly deteriorating.

Just to prove that football is a 'funny old game' (and would Jimmy Greaves had known that years later he would coin such a popular phrase?), England then beat Argentina 3-1 in front of 9,700 spectators at the same stadium two days later. Suddenly the spartan and deserted training camp (if that's what it could be called) didn't seem so depressing after all. The final game, against Bulgaria, must have depressed anyone who was within 20 miles of the stadium. It takes journalist Norman Giller to explain adequately:

> This was without question the most boring, sterile match England have ever contested. They needed only a draw to qualify for the quarter-finals ahead of Argentina and, as Bulgaria showed no inclination to win the match, England were content to sit back and make sure there were no mistakes. The result was that the ball hardly left the midfield area and neither goalkeeper was tested. A crowd of barely 6,000 watched the non-event ... but the Bulgarians did not manage a single serious goal attempt and England were little better.

No matter. England had reached the knockout stage, where they would play the world champions, Brazil. Three days later, in Vina del Mar, and after only two days of acclimatisation, England prepared for what was the most important game of Jimmy's career up until that point. The location was back at sea level, and their hotel overlooked a panoramic view of the bay and sea. Brazil had been playing there throughout the tournament, whereas England had the lengthy and tedious journey, plus the difference in altitude to contend with. It was at least an improvement on their barely adequate training camp, but so little time gave them minimal chance. They were not excuses, though, as Brazil, despite being without Pelé, ran out comfortable 3-1 winners in front of 17,000 fans (mostly cheering on Brazil). Brazil went on to win the World Cup and successfully defend the trophy they'd won four years earlier. England said goodbye at the quarter-final stage, something which became depressingly regular in the years that followed.

It was goodbye to South America and, to prove how haphazard the organisation was, a lot of the England players made their own way home (paid for by the FA), whilst Jimmy and Bobby Charlton travelled together and stopped off in New York for some sightseeing. They stayed a few days, visiting Central Park and Times Square, as well as taking a trip up the Empire State Building, and then made their way back to England. There were no supporters to greet them off the plane, no television cameras and no press reporters. There was no such invention in 1962 as satellite coverage, so the television highlights shown on the BBC were recordings screened 48 hours after the games, making the impact of the tournament even more negligible. It was almost as if it had never happened. Once again, different times.

Chapter Eight:

Swinging Sixties and all that

THE ENGLAND that Jimmy returned to at the end of the summer of 1962 was an ever-changing one. It was the start of the 'Swinging Sixties', a phenomenon which most people now agree only seemed to take place in London. Teenagers had suddenly found a freedom their parents had not had, especially those who were still relatively young during the Second World War. A new type of music was sweeping the nation, with The Beatles and The Rolling Stones in particular, exporting the 'British wave' across to the United States.

Fashions were changing. From the greyness of the 1950s, suddenly technicolour abounded and it was shown in the mini skirts of the girls and the shirts of the boys. The unquestioning belief in the authority of the government ended with the Profumo scandal in 1963, changing forever the relationship between politicians and the people. Britain was like a butterfly which had been cocooned inside for years after the war and now, as the exciting decade got into full swing, it emerged and gracefully spread its wings and blossomed. Most of it happened in London, though.

In Blackpool, things didn't change, but they didn't need to. The town was still the summer magnet for thousands of tourists, who arrived by train, by coach, by charabanc still and, for the lucky few, by car. The guest houses, offering 'full breakfast' and a teasmade in the room, were full to capacity. Landladies, the scourge of the under-demanding guests, made enough money to depart the cold winter and started to explore the delights of warmer climes. The guests just enjoyed their two weeks' holidays or the 'wakes week', which still existed in the northern towns of Wigan, Bolton and Burnley.

The promenade was packed. Any black-and-white photograph of the time encapsulates the Blackpool of the early 1960s. The beach is full, with hundreds of deckchairs randomly placed, father, wearing shirtsleeves and braces, asleep, mother with her knitting and children building a sandcastle. Donkeys carried excited holidaymakers whilst the ice cream vans had queues for as far as the eye could see. Britain's most successful seaside resort living up to its title.

Cafes offered pots of tea for the beach and bingo halls played to hundreds hoping for the £5 prize that attracted them in the first place. At the south end of the town, the Pleasure Beach – the original inspiration for Disneyland in California – introduced the new Alice in Wonderland ride and had a laughing clown that scared the children. The tower looked down in all of its majesty, with only the very brave daring the rickety lift that took visitors to the top. Blackpool was a summer resort and it still hasn't changed.

The problem with a town that conducts its affairs for just one group of people, such as tourists, is that the locals feel like they've been ignored and left behind. As now, the Blackpool of the 1960s was a black spot for unemployment and, so, the fortunes of the football club became ever more important. The weekly release from the misery of poverty was seen at Bloomfield Road. Unfortunately, Blackpool FC weren't willing to help their cause or ease their burden.

The club was in freefall, although two seasons of mid-table mediocrity didn't really show it. The team from a decade ago had gone and Ron Suart's thankless task was to try and keep Blackpool relevant, and also try and keep them in the top flight of English football. The fact that they managed to stay there until 1967 is a testament to the sheer bloody-mindedness of everyone connected to the club. Ray Charnley was scoring the goals and Jimmy Armfield was marshalling the team as captain. There were few successes and many frustrations. The only hint of any glory was a two-legged League Cup semi-final against Norwich City in a tournament that was only a couple of years old. They lost 4-3 on aggregate but few who turned up cared. There wasn't even a Wembley date to look forward to, as the final was over two legs anyway.

By this time, Jimmy was a world-class player. After the 1962 World Cup, he'd been acclaimed as the best right-back in the world and for the next three years was voted the best right-back in Europe. Any club would have loved him in their defence but there seems little evidence that clubs came calling. Today, a player of Jimmy's calibre would be the subject of numerous high bids and would be a major transfer target but things were different then. A look at Blackpool's transfer activity in the 1962/63 season sees just five players involved. Two in – John

McPhee and Pat Quinn (both from Motherwell) – and three out. The following season, only three players either departed or arrived. It's with that background knowledge that we can explain why Jimmy was able to stay loyal to the town he loved. There was no suggestion that he would leave and there was certainly no temptation from bigger clubs. His family were settled, his two sons were growing up in a place they loved and Jimmy was at the height of his playing success. All he needed now was to win the World Cup with England, and surely that would happen.

Chapter Nine:

The Ramsey revolution

AFTER THE disappointment of the 1962 World Cup in Chile, Walter Winterbottom was replaced as manager by Alf Ramsey. He hadn't been sacked, but resigned, probably sensing that the winds of change were about him at the FA headquarters. He'd been extremely successful, taking over as England's first full-time manager and serving for an incredible 16 seasons. In that time, his England team won 78 of their 139 games and only lost six at Wembley (although one of those was the infamous 6-3 defeat to Hungary when four Blackpool players wore the white of England). England had qualified for all four World Cups during his tenure and won the British Championship 13 times. It wasn't enough, though, and a replacement was found.

Winterbottom's experience in football prior to becoming England manager was a brief playing career with Manchester United, which was prematurely ended by injury. In contrast, Alf Ramsey had enjoyed an extensive and successful playing and managerial career before being appointed. He'd played for England 32 times and, as a manager, had taken the smalltown club of Ipswich Town from the bottom of the Third Division South to the First Division title in 1962 in just seven years. He was highly regarded but had his own ideas as to how to manage the national team. He became England manager on his own terms.

Winterbottom wasn't able to pick his teams, as that was decided by a committee (something which seems incredible today). In the latter stages of his tenure, he did pretty much have the final say but Ramsey wanted nothing to do with the old system and insisted that he alone would decide who would play and who wouldn't. Winterbottom had also been the FA director of coaching with overall responsibility for coaching nationwide. Ramsey preferred to concentrate on managing the national team. He was fiercely patriotic and his reluctance to engage with the press meant he was loved by his players and many supporters but seemingly disliked by sections of the media from an early stage. Years later, when he finally left the job, there are numerous stories of certain reporters running through the corridors of Wembley shouting in delight! He refused to criticise his players in public and certainly didn't enjoy the press conferences that were now becoming part of the game. He was a manager who Jimmy Armfield immediately bonded with and possibly the one who Jimmy admired above all others.

In his autobiography, Jimmy said that he and Alf had effectively become friends and often the manager would seek out the captain for his views on players and tactics. This might not sound unusual but this was an Alf Ramsey who was authoritarian in the dressing room and, at times, rather aloof, too. Managers and players were never really expected to be friends, although the Don Revie era at Leeds United certainly took that route, as we will see, but if a manager needed an ally in the dressing room, then the captain was the obvious person.

Jimmy's first match under Ramsey – and his first game as captain under the new manager – was away to France in the second leg of a European Nations Cup first-round tie. England, like many other top European countries, had refused to enter the inaugural tournament in 1960, so this was an attempt to qualify for the 1964 tournament. Jimmy had played in the 1-1 first-leg draw at Hillsborough, plus the two Home Championship games against Northern Ireland away (won 3-1) and Wales at home (won 4-0). The significance of the Wales game was that it was Winterbottom's last game and that only 27,500 attended. That was a record low for an England international at Wembley.

On to France for Ramsey's first match, at which stage he was still also managing relegation-threatened Ipswich Town and the selection committee was still operating. The game at the Parc des Princes was an absolute disaster, with England suffering a 5-2 defeat and being eliminated at the preliminary stage. Not a great start but if there were any excuses, they were that it was snowing heavily, the floodlights weren't very strong and a very small crowd turned up. Also, star midfielder Johnny Haynes was missing after breaking his leg in a car crash and, as mentioned, Ramsey was yet to assume total control of team selection. Jimmy recalled that he had an hour-long conversation with Ramsey at the airport after the game, where it was clear the new manager wasn't impressed with the team's performance. As he said as they boarded the plane: 'We don't want any more performances like that.' Probably an understatement of understatements.

Unfortunately, the second game under Ramsey wasn't any better. In the final Home Championship fixture of the season, they were beaten at Wembley 2-1 by Scotland. Gordon Banks made his debut and Jimmy was responsible for the opening goal for the Scots. He'd tried to play the ball out from his own box but was tackled and looked on in horror as Jim Baxter easily scored. There was a crowd of 98,000 who enjoyed far more comfort than in the past, as Wembley had caught up with the world by offering a roof that ran around the entire stadium and sheltered the stands from the elements. Things could only get better for the team, though, with the World Cup on the horizon. No panic. No questions but a determination that things would soon be back on track.

Thankfully, they were. A few weeks later, in the first game which saw Ramsey assume total control of team selection, England drew 1-1 at Wembley against Brazil. No Pelé, admittedly, but there was a Pepe, who scored an amazing 25-yard 'banana kick' free kick. Gordon Banks said that if it hadn't have hit the netting, the ball would have 'done a circular tour of the stadium'. Underneath the new roof, that would certainly have been a sight.

There then followed a three-match summer tour, with a 4-2 win against Czechoslovakia (although Jimmy didn't play due to an injured toe), a 2-1 win against East Germany and an 8-1 thrashing of what was regarded as a decent Switzerland side. That last game was notable for the one and only international appearance of Tony Kay. He was later caught up in the betting scandal from his days at Sheffield Wednesday and was subsequently imprisoned.

There seemed to be little that could now stop England and, of course, Jimmy from making a real stride forward towards the 1966 World Cup. The team were playing well, with Ramsey changing and trialling new players at the highest possible level. Jimmy retained his role as captain and had the respect of the players and, just as importantly, the manager. It was around this time that Ramsey made the promise that England would win the cup. That seemed brave, to say the least, but when Jimmy was asked for his view, he was, of course, a little more circumspect. 'Slight' was his response when asked what the chances were of England lifting the trophy. Maybe he was trying to dampen the expectation that was beginning to match the enthusiasm as the tournament drew ever closer.

The next two months saw England play and win three games. A 4-0 away win against Wales in the Home Championship, in which Bobby Charlton scored his 31st England goal to overtake Tom Finney and Nat Lofthouse's national scoring record, a 2-1 Wembley win over the Rest of the World to celebrate the FA's centenary and an 8-3 thrashing of Northern Ireland. That last game, in the British Championship, was the first full match played under the Wembley floodlights, but the performance was in itself enough to shine a light on the 55,000 crowd. A much larger attendance of 133,000 was at Hampden Park six months later to see England lose to Scotland again, the first time they'd lost three in a row in this fixture for more than 80 years. The score was 1-0 but this was an unusually subdued performance and, despite it being the first defeat after six consecutive victories, Ramsey was not pleased at all. Still, 1964 was going to be busy for England and their captain, Jimmy Armfield. There were fixtures planned against Uruguay, Portugal, the Republic of Ireland and the USA, followed by a 'Little World Cup' in Brazil against the world champions, Argentina and Portugal. It would be a meaningful test for England and it would be more captaincy experience for Jimmy Armfield. Sadly, Jimmy didn't play in any of them.

Chapter Ten:

Injury, recovery and a dream destroyed

IT'S A testament to Jimmy's faith and lack of bitterness that the date 25 April 1964 was never one that stayed with him. It didn't dig into his consciousness or eat away in his waking hours or give him sleepless nights. He never bemoaned his fate and he never looked back at what could have been. Few of us would have that self-discipline not to rage against the injustice of life. Jimmy had that self-control. It says more about him than can really be put into words here. On that Saturday afternoon at Ipswich Town's Portman Road, Jimmy Armfield's international career was effectively ended and his personal hopes of World Cup glory were wrecked, too.

It was a nothing game or, in tennis terminology, a dead rubber. The final match of the season, Blackpool well clear of relegation, although finishing in 18th position, at an already relegated Ipswich Town. In the stands was Ipswich's former manager and the current England boss, Alf Ramsey. He was there to meet his captain, as the two were due to travel to London immediately after the game to join up with the rest of the England squad in preparation for the match with Uruguay.

The game was actually an entertaining 4-3 victory for the home side, one of those end-of-season matches that crop up occasionally when the two teams, who have struggled all season to play with a flourish or achieve success, suddenly find the freedom to show their fans what could have been. Sadly, Jimmy only played for around 20 minutes.

Midway through the first half, without an opposing player near him, he felt a sharp and acute pain in his left groin. It was so bad that he had to leave the field immediately, unable to carry on. There was no obvious cause, it just happened. He waited in the dressing room until the game was over before travelling back to Blackpool, where he was immediately taken to hospital. There, it was diagnosed as a severely torn groin muscle, the type of injury that had ended Tom Finney's career. Ramsey had come to see him at half-time and realised immediately that his captain would not be playing for England again anytime soon or maybe even for Blackpool. It was serious.

Today, such an injury would not be regarded as career-threatening but in the 1960s the medical world hadn't quite caught up with the dangers professional sportsmen and women faced. The only advice he could receive was to rest, try some very gentle jogging and to swim regularly. It is a testament to his commitment that just four months later he lined up at Turf Moor against Burnley for the opening game of the new season. Unfortunately, the England boat was sailing away and he wasn't on it. Jimmy missed the next 23 England international games while Bobby Moore took over the captaincy and Jack Charlton and George Cohen became mainstays of the defence, the latter in Jimmy's favourite right-back position. Despite Jimmy playing

81 times for Blackpool between the end of the 1963/64 season until the end of the 1965/66 season, he didn't represent his country in that time.

Looking back, it seems cruel that Ramsey should seemingly discard his captain, particularly as Jimmy was back at his best for the ever-struggling Blackpool side. One of the top coaches in the English game, Malcolm Allison, was particularly critical of the manager concerning Jimmy's absence but Ramsey was only interested in one thing and that was winning the World Cup. Sentiment played no part in his decisions. He had publicly stated that the World Cup would be won by England in 1966 and now he had to back that up by putting together the best players to wear the shirt in the build-up and in the tournament itself. Jimmy wasn't one of them at that time, at least according to Ramsey. It looked over but then, in March 1966, after a goalless draw at Arsenal, the England manager went to see him in the Blackpool dressing room and asked if he wanted to return to international duty. The answer was a definite yes! One can only imagine the excitement that Jimmy must have felt, especially as the World Cup was looming. Maybe he would play in it after all? There was hope but then sometimes it's the hope that lets you down.

Unbeknown to Jimmy, Ramsey had watched him in a few Blackpool games and had been impressed as to how he had recovered from the injury and how he appeared to have returned to his best form. George Cohen had made the right-back position his own over the previous two years but having Jimmy back would be a bonus. So, it was with a great deal of relief – but apprehension, too – that Jimmy put on the white shirt and stepped out at Wembley in front of 55,000 fans on 4 May 1966. The opponents were Yugoslavia and it was the last England game under the Twin Towers before the World Cup started. They won 2-0 and Jimmy received praise for the way he marked the teenage sensation Dragan Džajić. Now it was a case of seeing if he could replace Cohen in Ramsey's footballing affections.

Jimmy made the final 22-man England squad for the World Cup, although he was unsure as to who would be the starting right-back. All he could do now was to play as well as he could in the four-match tour of Scandinavia and Poland, if he was chosen. He was. For the opening game on 26 June, he kept his place at right-back and, with Bobby Moore rested, was captain. England won comfortably, by 3-0, and fellow Blackpool man Alan Ball even missed a penalty. Jimmy played well and almost scored at the end, which would have certainly helped his cause, but, as at Portman Road two years earlier, fate played its most unkind hand once again.

With five minutes to go, Jimmy was clattered by one of their midfield players, who stamped on his left foot. It was clumsy, if not deliberate, but X-rays after the game showed that he had broken his little toe, and that was that. Jimmy couldn't play against Norway, Denmark or Poland and George Cohen regained and kept his place at right-back throughout the tour and, of course, the World Cup tournament. Jimmy's dream was over.

It's at moments like this when you have to look deep into your soul and find a way to deal with the crushing disappointment. Jimmy never really explained how he must have felt in those dark days, as that was clearly very private, but surely there must have been moments when he inwardly raged? It's more than likely that his faith kept him going and as Jimmy was the kind of man who would prefer to stay silent as opposed to saying something unpleasant, his private thoughts were always kept to himself.

Of course, Jimmy did talk publicly about how he was proud to be part of the whole England set-up during the victorious tournament but there was always the question as to whether Ramsey would have picked him ahead of Cohen anyway? It was never asked, lost amongst far more celebratory moments, but the answer possibly may not have been to Jimmy's liking. As it was, George Cohen played exceptionally well throughout the World Cup.

Jimmy did play a part for England, though. After all, he was still in the playing squad and his toe had recovered but it was clear that Ramsey had effectively chosen his best XI. At the start of the tournament, Jimmy read a lesson at Westminster Abbey, with all the players present, and he became an unofficial ambassador for England. He was chosen to look after the 'reserves' as they had been rather cruelly dubbed, even managing them to a 3-1 victory over an Arsenal team that hadn't returned to full training, and it was sure that he gave Alf as much advice as he could, without interfering.

What of the final, though? The story of that day is etched in every England supporter's mind but the hard luck stories didn't just include Jimmy, but Jimmy Greaves, too. Having missed the quarter-final and semi-final with a gashed shin, he was not recalled for the final and took it badly. It seemed to haunt him. On 30 July, a hot and balmy day, Jimmy and all the other reserves sat in the stands watching with the fans. Ramsey had asked him to bring the players down to the team bench with about two minutes of the 90 to go, which Jimmy did. That, of course, meant they all missed West Germany's equaliser! Thankfully, extra time was a little more enjoyable. Once the game was over, the celebrations started but it was an awkward time for him and the others who had been forced to watch instead of playing. With the red-shirted players enjoying a lap of honour, Jimmy returned to the dressing room and waited for the trophy.

He played his part in all the post-match celebrations, though, and was interviewed extensively, especially about his enforced absence. There was no winner's medal, as FIFA didn't think of such things for non-playing squad members. Thankfully, that would be rectified decades later. Jimmy did receive his £1,000 share of the squad's bonus and his FA international match fees, which in those days was quite a lot of money, but his England career was over after 44 caps, 15 of them as captain. I'll leave it to Jimmy to explain his feelings on that wonderful day for England:

I would be lying if I pretended that on Saturday, 30 July 1966, I wasn't wishing I could be out there on the field instead of sitting in the stands … I've been asked this so many times to describe how the reserves felt and it isn't easy. It was the greatest day in the history of English football and it was impossible not feel a sense of deep frustration. Generations of football supporters can reel off the 11 names of England's heroes … and those names are there in the record books for all time but, apart from a few, how many people can remember the 11 who missed out? I'm not bitter, I'm genuinely not, but there are times when you just shake your head and wonder.

There is little to add to that, except to say that, as the years rolled by, the two Jimmys, Armfield and Greaves, became the most famous of the ones who didn't play. It was reminiscent of the great racing driver Stirling Moss who, despite his many successes on the track, never became Formula One world champion. Moss later said that it made him even more famous for finishing second on so many occasions, instead of becoming another of the many drivers who had won the title. It wasn't quite the same with Jimmy Armfield but the dignity he showed when constantly asked about it made him an even more loved character in the sport.

Chapter 11:

The Tangerine dream fades

ALTHOUGH THERE was no official announcement, Jimmy Armfield's international career had come to an end and now it was a case of concentrating on his club. England were world champions and, so, were the one team that the rest wanted to beat. The XI who played on that momentous day were effectively automatically on every teamsheet. Alf Ramsey had found his winning formula and was reluctant to change it. Jimmy returned to Blackpool, where things weren't quite as good.

There was no suggestion that he would move elsewhere, so he had to make a personal decision as to how long he wanted to keep on playing. Blackpool's rapid decline played a large part in his deliberations. Just a month after that sultry day at Wembley, the 1966/67 English football season started. Virtually every supporter in the country approached the new campaign with excitement and vigour. Crowds boomed, the sun shone constantly and football was back in fashion. Everywhere but Blackpool, sadly.

Alan 'running himself daft' Ball (the subject of the second most famous piece of commentary from Kenneth Wolstenholme on World Cup Final day) had been sold to Everton for a British record fee of £115,000 and Blackpool were running on empty, even before the season started. Everton were bigger, more ambitious and had more money. A talent like Ball couldn't be expected to stay at a relatively small club and his departure was inevitable after the Wembley glory day. So, whilst fans flocked to their respective football grounds with a skip in their step, a song in their heart and a hope in their soul, Blackpool fans trudged disconsolately to Bloomfield Road in fewer numbers than before to witness a season of utter desperation.

It's not really known what Jimmy made of that catastrophic season but by the time the first home game against Leicester City came around, Blackpool had already been on the receiving end of a thrashing at Sheffield Wednesday. They won just six times all season, only one at home, but two on Merseyside, which gave rise to the curious statistic that they won more games in Liverpool than Blackpool! The other curious fact of that truly dreadful season was that the one home victory was against Newcastle United and by six goals to nil! How on earth the Magpies allowed that to happen, will always remain a mystery. It was the game that saw a certain Alan Suddick shine for the opposition and he was immediately signed by Blackpool and became one of the most loved of players at Bloomfield Road by the supporters. It didn't really help in that campaign, though. By the end of the season, a crowd of 6,000 had been recorded and the average of 17,000 was the lowest in the First Division, some 3,000 fewer than the next lowest at Burnley. The final tally of 21 points meant they finished bottom, some 12 points from safety, and Blackpool's 56 successive years of First Division football were at an end. The World Cup hadn't been kind to Jimmy or Blackpool!

They were back in the Second Division for the first time since the mid-1930s and for Jimmy it was a new experience playing at a lower level. It is to his enormous credit and a sign of his loyalty that he carried on playing, despite becoming more and more affected by niggling injuries. He was 32, an age at which many footballers retired or were forced out of the game due to their bodies struggling with the pressure, but Jimmy carried on. Why? It was probably because he loved Blackpool, he wanted to see them get back to the top again, and mainly because he just still loved playing football. His commitment must have been tested in that first season in the Second Division, though.

Ron Suart had left and former playing legend Stan Mortensen was the new manager at Blackpool. There could not have been a more popular choice amongst the supporters, his hat-trick still standing as the only one in an FA Cup Final. Today, he is regarded as the greatest player Blackpool has produced and even in the late 1960s his legendary status was being built and expanded. He returned to the club and immediately started to rebuild the team, signing the incredible talent of Tony Green and the lanky and tricky Tommy Hutchison, both from lower league Scottish clubs. Blackpool's star started to shine again.

They'd spent the season battling for promotion with both Ipswich Town and Queens Park Rangers and, after winning six in a row, it was a last-match trip to Leeds Road for the season-deciding battle with Huddersfield Town. Few of the 3,000 or so Blackpool fans who attended on that grey and misty day will forget the sequence of events.

Blackpool won 3-1, quite comfortably, and the fans ran on to the pitch in celebration, convinced that an immediate return to the top tier had been attained. Sadly, the cheers of joy became whispers of concern and then howls of anguish as bad news filtered through on handheld transistors and by word-of-mouth. In the other deciding game, an Aston Villa defender had scored an own goal with a few minutes remaining and QPR had won 2-1. It meant that the London club would grace the First Division for the first time in their history, pipping Blackpool by 0.21 of a goal at a time when goal average was the decider. Having said that, even if goal difference had been the final arbiter, Blackpool would still have finished third.

It was cruel and it remains the highest number of points – in a two points-per-win era – that a team collected without gaining promotion. 'Morty' was calm and reassuring and, after the game, he took the team to the George Hotel in Huddersfield. This place has a certain amount of notoriety, as it is where the game of rugby league was founded! That wasn't actually on anyone's minds at that time and, as captain, Jimmy had to give encouragement to the players. He basically told them to remain positive and that they were good enough to win the title the following season. Words of comfort and hope but how much more disappointment could he take? Nearly a year on from the country's most famous footballing victory, with Jimmy sat watching, he now had to see the glory of promotion ripped away from him, as it disappeared into Shepherd's Bush.

Jimmy kept playing, despite his prophecy not coming true. Blackpool floundered, finishing well out of the promotion race, and Mortensen was inexplicably sacked by a nervous board of directors. It made no sense to the fans and it certainly made no sense to someone as morally loyal as Jimmy Armfield. As he said many times, he had no idea what 'Morty' had done wrong.

A new manager, in Les Shannon, and a new way of playing followed. Despite the loss of the talent that was Tony Green due to injury, Blackpool kept up the promotion pressure all season and were elevated back to the First Division on a Monday night at, of all places, Preston North End. Jimmy often said that it was that match when the rivalry between the two clubs, and ultimately the supporters, started. The night of 13 April 1970 saw Deepdale packed with anything between 30,000 and 38,000 fans, depending on which figures you believe. That also included anything between 15,000 and 20,000 Blackpool fans, both inside and outside the ground. It wasn't just that the men in tangerine could be promoted but Preston were fighting an ultimately unsuccessful attempt to avoid relegation. Blackpool won 3-0 with a hat-trick from former Blackburn Rovers man Fred Pickering and were promoted back to the First Division after three years. Five days later, Preston were officially relegated to the Third Division.

It was a night of celebration but neither Jimmy nor any of the Blackpool players toasted their success with champagne. It was felt that the two clubs were so close that celebrating your own success at the expense of your neighbours was not the right thing to do. Jimmy certainly didn't see Preston North End as bitter rivals in those days, as many fans would watch both teams on alternate weekends. That would be inconceivable today, of course, as the Fylde Coast derby is now eagerly awaited, although the number of times the two clubs have found themselves in the same division has decreased over the years.

One of the personal stories lost during this season involving Jimmy was the injury to the new 'wonderkid' Tony Green. He was clearly a star for the future and had already attracted the attention of bigger clubs but he had suffered a terrible injury and was effectively out of action for the entire promotion season. It meant long stays in hospital whilst his Achillies healed and it was at this time that Jimmy would regularly turn up announced at Tony's home and take on babysitting duties so that Tony's wife, Christine, could visit her husband in hospital. As Tony explained to me, they weren't necessarily friends outside of football, but team-mates, but this was the kind of selfless and generous thing that just came naturally to Jimmy. Sadly, for Tony Green, he suffered a career-ending injury in September 1972 whilst a Newcastle United player and was forced to retire from the game at the age of just 25.

The promotion game at Deepdale has now become legendary among modern-day Blackpool supporters, despite the fact that few of them attended or were even alive at the time, but for Jimmy, it was just another game, albeit with a successful outcome. He probably knew that it would be the last time he would taste any kind of success playing for Blackpool and his club career hadn't exactly showered him with glittering prizes, the club's achievements failing to match the ability of the man himself. He had already made the decision to retire after the following season and Blackpool's return to the highest level in English football was as disastrous as the previous time they'd been there. Jimmy's body was failing him. A bad knee injury was refusing to heal and he was finding it more and more difficult to do the things that came so naturally on a football field. Despite that, he was still ranked as one of the best defenders in the English game and the chance to play at the top for one last season was something he deserved and something he was determined to enjoy. The First Division was like 'strawberries without cream', according to a player back in the 1930s. Now, the strawberries were fresh and the cream was sweet. Blackpool and Jimmy were back.

Chapter 12:

Farewell to the tangerine shirt

JIMMY'S FINAL season of his playing career could not have been more frustrating. He actually only played 28 times due to his knee injury and hardly ever ended up on the winning side. Blackpool were completely unprepared for a return to the First Division and what was effectively the same squad struggled to compete despite boasting Tony Green, Mickey Burns, Tommy Hutchison and Jimmy. It proved that the gulf in class between the top two leagues in England was as wide as ever. They won a couple of games early on but then went on a 35-match run without another league victory. This included an astonishing home game against Chelsea on 24 October when, beyond all expectations, Blackpool were three up at half-time against the boys from the fashionable part of London. Not only did they not win from that position, they somehow contrived to lose 4-3 with a last-minute own goal from Dave Hatton. It was ineptitude of the highest order and, two days later, manager Les Shannon was sacked. It was left to Jimmy to try and keep the players' morale high whilst waiting for a replacement. That replacement was Bob Stokoe, who arrived in December 1970 with the team in the bottom two and, despite his best efforts, that's where they remained until the end of the season.

Jimmy hadn't completely decided to quit at that stage but he did persuade the club to give him a testimonial game on 21 September at Bloomfield Road. Persuade is the right word because, astonishingly, they weren't remotely keen to begin with! Chairman William Cartmell, not exactly the most popular of people in the long history of a club that has seen a number of unpopular personalities, at first refused, as it was during the Illuminations period. Why that should be a problem wasn't explained but why Jimmy had to fight for his testimonial is something that needed, but didn't get, an explanation. Eventually, Cartmell relented and persuaded his fellow board members to back the idea but Jimmy had to find the sponsorship for the souvenir programme and arrange for the opposing players. Even looking at this today, in an age when testimonials are hardly thought of and the very word seems to belong to another era, this seems incredible. Players weren't paid an enormous amount in those days, so a testimonial for a long-serving employee like Jimmy should have been a 'given' and not resented. As Jimmy said in his autobiography: 'I'd played almost 600 matches and I was due a testimonial. I persisted and they eventually raised the subject again and agreed.'

The ground was made available free of charge (which surely seems the least the club could do) and a crowd of 17,000 turned up to see Blackpool take on a team that included Billy Bremner, Jack Charlton, Colin Bell, Francis Lee and Mike Summerbee. It raised around £6,000, which in 1970 was a significant amount of money and certainly more than Jimmy had been paid by the game. It was a success. Of course, it was. It was for Jimmy. At least he could retire knowing that he had a few pennies in the bank but the stunning lack of support from Blackpool Football Club did them few favours.

Bob Stokoe was regarded as one of the country's leading upcoming managers and his task at Blackpool was simple. He had to turn their fortunes around and, for that reason, he had to make some harsh and unpopular decisions. One of those was to tell Jimmy that he was no longer part of his first-team plans. He offered him a free transfer but Jimmy was never going to play for any other team apart from his beloved Blackpool. So, he refused and announced that his last game would be the final game of the season, at home to Manchester United on 1 May 1971.

For those of us who witnessed it, the moments leading up to kick-off were emotional. Both sets of players, Blackpool in tangerine and United in white, lined up to form a guard of honour to welcome him on to the pitch. It was a fitting tribute in front of a crowd of around 29,000. It's also worth noting, again, that if Jimmy was playing today, he would have been wearing a Manchester United shirt and not a Blackpool one. There surely would have been no set of circumstances that would not allow the lure of top-class football to overshadow his loyalty. Those were different days, though.

For the record, the game was a 1-1 draw and Blackpool finished at the bottom of the league and were relegated back to the Second Division. One month later, they won the second Anglo-Italian Cup by beating Bologna 2-1 in the final in Italy and picked up their first silverware since 1953. It was ironic, as Stokoe didn't even want the team to compete, as he had to rebuild the side, but the board had insisted and Blackpool went on to become the most successful club in the tournament's four-year existence. What was also ironic is that Jimmy had gone. Just as he had joined Blackpool when they were at their height, but was too late for the FA Cup Final glory, just as he failed to make the team for the 1966 World Cup Final, when he surely should have been there, he missed Blackpool's greatest moment for 18 years. It's a sad fact that, despite being one of England's greatest-ever players, the only thing he won was promotion in 1970.

He was the captain, though, and he was respected for that. Tony Green, who played with him during that final season explained that 'everything he said in the dressing-room was listened to. He never shouted, as he was a quiet speaker. The players listened because they respected him ... and what a player he was, too! That gets forgotten sometimes.'

Jimmy played 626 times for Blackpool and made the biggest number of league appearances for the club, with 568. A real 'one-club' man. It is never likely to be beaten. As he explained in *Blackpool Football* by Robert Daniels:

Retirement was a huge wrench. It was so difficult to come to terms with the knowledge that there was no way back, that I had made an irrevocable decision. At 35, my chosen career was over and I had never known anything else. My time clock had been set around Blackpool Football Club. I got up at eight, had a light breakfast, went to the ground and trained until lunchtime ... it was a set routine. Even when Duncan and John were babies, I would do the night feed with the bottle on Sunday, Monday and Tuesday and it would be my turn to do the sleeping for the rest of the week as Saturday approached. 'You're a long time finished' is a popular expression in football and, believe me, you are.

Chapter 13:

A new life ... where to now?

WHENEVER YOU lose something, or someone, that was important to you, the sense of emptiness can be overwhelming. One can only imagine Jimmy's feelings when he drove home after that final appearance in a tangerine shirt. His decision had been made and it was irreversible.

The routine that had served him so well down the years, with the regular trips to the training ground, the build-up to the matches and the resting of his body before playing, had now gone. He didn't need to do any of those things anymore. The question was, though, what on earth was he going to do now?

In the days before huge amounts of money flooded into the English game, players were nervous and apprehensive of the day they knew they could no longer play. Today, the top players around the world are usually financially secure from their early 20s but not so in Jimmy's era. He was never paid a fortune and, so, it was a case of looking for a new venture whilst deciding what to do with his life and also making sure that Anne didn't become irritated with his constant presence around the house!

Predictably, footballers would buy a public house or open a greengrocers. One of Jimmy's team-mates, the Welsh international Glyn James, opened a post office near to my childhood home and even the supremely talented Alan Suddick became a market stall holder in Blackpool town centre after he retired. What would Jimmy do? Well, thankfully, as well as being an excellent footballer on the field, he also had intelligence and the inner determination to make sure he could always take care of his family, Anne and the two boys. So, for that reason and when he was just 24 years of age, he decided that he would learn a trade outside of football and become a journalist.

It's an incredible decision, really. In 1959, Jimmy was playing for Blackpool and had just made his full England international debut. His career was at its height already and he could have been forgiven for thinking that life was easy and that nothing and no one could touch him. Look at players today and their casual attitude to the world around them as they climb into their Ferrari and return to their multi-million-pound house. They have no cares. Despite the comparative lack of wealth, Jimmy was a famous footballer, yet he thought differently. In 1959, in between dashing around the world packing his tangerine or white or red shirt to play football at the highest level, he also started to train to be a journalist.

For those who knew Jimmy, especially in his radio days, it's not something to wonder at. His choice of words, his eloquence, his master of the art of speaking, all were part of Jimmy Armfield. When he was younger, he used to love art and music, in particular, so it was hardly surprising that the written word should appeal to him. That was what made him approach the *Blackpool Evening Gazette* newspaper.

Like all local newspapers in those days, the *Gazette* was read avidly by the local population. It was, of course, in those pre-internet days, the only reliable source of reporting on the football match that many had witnessed, especially as the television cameras were rarely a visitor. It was a harsh training ground for a young man, never mind someone who already had a different career path laid out for him.

It was the sports editor of the newspaper, Cliff Greenwood, who gave Jimmy his first taste of what it was like to be a journalist and, in the long list of people who played a part in his remarkable life, Greenwood should have a place reserved at the very top. He was a blunt Yorkshireman (aren't they all?!) who had actually won a competition for *The People*, a national Sunday newspaper, with an article he'd written in under ten minutes. His break into the world of journalism was one of those almost ridiculous stories that just have to be true! He used to walk his dog at night in a field near his home in Lytham and every night he fed a horse he'd become fond of with an apple. It was then rumoured that there was a horse in the Lytham area that had been entered for the 1928 Grand National at Aintree and Cliff was asked if he knew anything about it. At the time, he was working as an errand boy for the *Gazette* and told the editor at the time that he would find out. Obviously, he had been told some time previously that the horse who was being fed nightly with apples from Cliff's garden, was the very same horse. Once Cliff gleefully announced to the impressed editor that he'd found the horse, his future at the paper was secured, as he clearly had the 'nose' of a journalist. He was then told to report daily on the horse's progress and was actually sent to Aintree to report on the race. Tipperary Tim, as the horse was called, won at odds of 100-1 and Cliff was made the racing correspondent for the *Gazette*.

He was the man who allowed Jimmy to come to the newspaper's offices three afternoons a week and watch and learn. With his own break into newspapers being as unique as possible, he probably saw that Jimmy could benefit in a similar way. Jimmy told the tale of how he bought an old typewriter for £2 and learned shorthand, although he never fully mastered that art. He soon became proficient at writing engaging and disciplined copy but that only came about after trial and error. After a few months, he was asked if he would start reporting on local football games, as having the great Jimmy Armfield attending amateur fixtures and reporting would certainly sell a few more copies. Jimmy agreed and so he became a regular reporter on the Blackpool Wednesday League.

Can you imagine this? Jimmy was playing for England and actually played in a World Cup. He was a regular in the Blackpool First Division side, yet here he was standing on the touchline, in all weathers, on a Wednesday night reporting on Layton Institute taking on the Fire Brigade. It was humble but, in a way, it defined Jimmy as a man more than virtually everything else. He knew he had to start at the bottom.

I compare this attitude to someone I experienced whilst I was working at the BBC. A former successful sportsman, who I won't name for obvious reasons, who wanted to be a television presenter. He arrived with a belief that it wouldn't be too difficult and sat in the presenter's chair ready to broadcast. It didn't happen, as he immediately announced that 'he wasn't here to write his own scripts' and expected his production team to do it for him. He didn't stay long. I certainly could never imagine Jimmy ever being so arrogant or, indeed, so foolish.

This is how Jimmy described his first reporting commission:

> There was a match between Victorians and the Police being played on a pitch in Crosland Road. I remember that I stood on the side in the pouring rain under an umbrella, trying to make notes. That wasn't easy, I can tell you that. Anyway, I managed somehow and went home straight afterwards and typed out my report. It had to be on Cliff's desk at eight in the morning. I was paid the princely sum of ten shillings, which wasn't much to be honest, but it was my first working wage outside of playing the game. Anyway, the articles became known as 'Armfield's Match' and they became quite popular. It was good fun and I'm pretty sure it worked wonders for the profile of the Wednesday League!

Different times, admittedly, but how many current Premier League players at the height of their game would be willing to stand on the touchline and watch, never mind report on, an amateur football match?

So, when Jimmy retired from playing in 1971, who should contact him but Cliff Greenwood and for a few months Jimmy got down to writing about his favourite passion – football. It seemed a natural transition for him. It meant he could still attend games, albeit at a very local level, and continue his love affair with the written word. It helped in a big way but there was still a burning ambition within him and that was to stay in the game. The question was ... how?

The answer was football management. After his disappointment during the 1966 World Cup, Alf Ramsey had always said that he would help Jimmy to move smoothly from playing to managing, should he be interested. He stayed true to his word and he chose Jimmy to be a player-manager for the Football Association tour of Tahiti, New Zealand and Hong Kong in 1969. It was a great honour and one that Jimmy took very seriously.

Nowadays, it's inconceivable that a team of top internationals would embark on a tour if they weren't playing for their country – or their club if it was a lucrative Asian tour – but in 1969 it was different. This wasn't an England team but it still included the likes of Don Megson, Alan Hodgkinson, Keith Weller, Tony Hateley and George Eastham, plus, of course, Jimmy Armfield.

The tour, in changeable weather conditions, to say the least, lasted a month. In that time, the representative side played and won 11 games, scoring 68 goals and conceding just seven. They'd played in the warm and welcoming atmosphere of New Zealand, where they beat the national side three times, the humidity of Tahiti and the hostile environment of Hong Kong, where a full-scale demonstration took place at the end of the game in which Jimmy came on as a substitute. It had nothing to do with football, as it was a political protest, but it was concerning enough for the players to dash straight off the pitch at the end of the game.

In Bangkok, Jimmy had his first real 'altercation' with the FA officials. After one of the games, he arranged for the players to return to the hotel immediately to shower, as the facilities at the ground were not sufficient. It was then that he met two of the FA councillors, Ike Robinson and Jack Bowers, who were less than impressed with the sight of Jimmy and the players lounging around the hotel reception in T-shirts and shorts. The fact that it was 93 degrees Fahrenheit (well before Celsius was part of the vocabulary) and the humidity was at its highest, didn't matter. The two officials were both dressed in suits and pullovers and even had a raincoat thrown over their arms, seemingly completely oblivious to the temperature and the conditions. It was a disagreement that Jimmy refused to budge on and later, when the report for the tour was released by the FA, Jimmy's role as manager was hardly referred to, except the words: 'I'm sure Jimmy Armfield has learned a lot on this tour.'

He *had* learned a lot from the tour, including a tetchy press conference in Hong Kong when one of the reporters suddenly realised that it wasn't the full England team that had come to play, but a representative one. The suggestion that Hong Kong was 'beneath' the World Cup winners was quickly deflected by Jimmy, who used his charm and diplomacy to avoid what was the beginning of a difficult interview. This wasn't helped by the fact that there were hardly any officials on the tour representing the FA. Jimmy had to do it all himself.

That was Jimmy's first taste of football management and, despite the typically authoritarian treatment from the FA, he wanted more. He decided he wanted to get into football management and, so, it came to pass. By the summer of 1971, he had transitioned from Blackpool player to Bolton Wanderers manager.

Chapter 14:

Management time ...

IT'S NOT clear whether Jimmy went looking for a management opportunity or if he was sought out by interested clubs but it was inevitable that the man who captained both Blackpool and England so many times would soon find a club. There was surely no way he wouldn't stay involved in the game.

Most new managers tend to get their chance at a lower league or smaller club, but Jimmy was almost immediately contacted by Blackburn Rovers, who, although languishing in the Third Division, were big enough to be an attractive proposition. A club of great historic standing and one that had lofty ambitions to return to the top of the English game. It was their chairman, Bill Bancroft, and manager, Johnny Carey, who unexpectedly turned up on his doorstep one day with the intention of signing Jimmy as a player. That was never going to happen, as Jimmy's knee was no longer up to the physical strain of football and he had little appetite for playing for anyone else but Blackpool, but then the conversation changed. Carey had left to return to training but Bancroft stayed and offered Jimmy the opportunity of becoming manager at the club. It was a great offer but, for reasons Jimmy never explained and maybe he didn't fully understand himself, he politely declined, promising to let them know should he change his mind.

A few days later, Bolton Wanderers came calling – literally. All roads seem to have led to Jimmy's front door and this time he accepted the role. Why Bolton over Blackburn? It's difficult to see now, as the Trotters had just been relegated to the Third Division for the first time in their history and he would be replacing the legendary Nat Lofthouse as manager. It seems he had an instant rapport with the chairman, Jack Banks, who was a self-made millionaire and had a very direct way of speaking. To use the well-worn phrase, he called 'a spade a spade'. He also spoke to Lofthouse, who obviously sold the club in glowing terms to Jimmy, despite their recent on-field problems.

Jimmy accepted the job and, on 1 August 1971, he became manager of one of the most famous clubs in England (alongside their 1953 nemesis Blackpool) with just 13 days until the start of the new season. There was a lot of work to do.

In 1971, Bolton was an archetypal northern town. Still immersed in the cotton industry, which had brought about its wealth, the pre-boundary change Lancashire town was exactly what you would expect if you were looking for 'northernness'. On the outskirts of the city of Manchester, it retained its independence, its buildings and environment, a mixture of old and grimy and new and clean. Families still lived in rows of brown brick terraced houses, with gloomy alleys behind. The huge mills dominated the skyline, with most of the employment based there, and the centre was a snapshot of a 1970 postcard, with outdoor and indoor markets competing with the department stores that have now long gone. It was both grim and exciting, with new dual carriageways ready to expand and separate the old town. Bolton was as northern as you could get. It also boasted a famous football club that, like many places in similar situations, had a passionate and loyal fanbase. Like Blackpool, Bolton Wanderers were a club who were screaming to be released from mediocrity and taken back to the top of the English footballing pyramid.

Jimmy didn't relocate his family once he'd made the decision to take the job. A walk around the streets one day made that decision for him. It wasn't that he didn't like what he saw. After all, there was a grittiness about the people that he identified with but it was just not a part of the country where he wanted to uproot his wife and boys to. Maybe it reminded him of his birthplace, Denton? He later felt the same when he moved to Leeds. So, instead, he decided he would make the daily pre-M55 90-minute commute from Blackpool each day, so as to make sure his family were still secure in the place they loved. As Duncan said: 'We always came first.'

In a way, Bolton Wanderers mirrored the town in 1971. They were a club similar to Blackpool in that the supporters were part of it, in what today would be described as a 'community club'. They lived for Saturdays and Burnden Park but the club's fortunes had waned badly and it was a Third Division Bolton Wanderers that Jimmy walked into. The ground, able to hold more than 40,000 spectators, was in dire need of some tender loving care. Like most grounds in England in the 1970s (Bloomfield Road included), it was a mixture of huge terraces with metal barriers, a few stands with seats for the wealthier fans and a pitch that looked like it had been ploughed on a daily basis. They didn't even have an official training ground, so the players had to jog to a nearby field or use the perimeter track to work out on.

Jimmy wasn't initially convinced that taking the Bolton job was a good idea. Not because he didn't feel they were a good club but because he wasn't sure if he was up to the task at the beginning of his managerial career. A call to and then a meeting with Manchester United's Matt Busby convinced him to go ahead. Busby, who had achieved so much, basically told him to take it and find out how good or bad he was going to be. It was a wise piece of advice.

There were only two weeks until the start of the season and many things had to be arranged. One of the first things he did was not necessarily that important but it immediately registered with the fans. He made sure the team would play in their traditional colours of white shirts and blue shorts, replacing the all-white kit they had adopted. It wasn't due to any superstitions on his part, as Bolton had really hit hard times at that point, but more to do with understanding the needs of the supporters. It was a small decision but immediately guaranteed the fans would be on his side. It also proved that Jimmy understood the fans and the impact the club has on a local community. He was instantly popular!

One of his initial duties was to arrange a couple of pre-season friendlies and this is where he really understood how much his professional, and personal, life had changed. Suddenly, he wasn't 'one of the lads' and decisions were now being made by him and him alone. Travel arrangements were made by him.

Player contracts were made by him. Player transfers were made by him. Training was taken by him. It almost immediately meant very long hours in the office and very little time at home. It was part of a manager's job!

In the few weeks before the season (he'd actually had the opportunity of seeing the players earlier, as he had agreed to take over as manager some time before he actually signed), he met the squad properly and had to make harsh and unpopular decisions over whether he wanted them at the club or not. For someone who had always had these things done to him, he made sure he made any personal decision about a player's future in the kindest and most gentle of ways. It was Jimmy's style but it was also him as a decent human being. He became instantly popular with the players but he made sure there was a distance between himself and them. He was, after all, now the manager.

The squad was a strong one for the Third Division, with the experience of the likes of Gareth Williams, Warwick Rimmer and Allan Boswell alongside the youth and potential of Peter Reid, Barry Siddall and Sam Allardyce. They were one of the favourites for an immediate return to the Second Division and the fans flocked to Burnden Park, all seeing a bright new dawn after the sun had set on the era of Nat Lofthouse.

In their opening league and League Cup fixtures, Bolton won five and drew five, losing just once, to York City at home. Then they were drawn at home to Manchester City in the third round of the League Cup, with Mike Summerbee, Francis Lee and Colin Bell ready to show the Trotters that they were nowhere near ready enough to compete at a higher level than the third tier. It didn't quite go according to City's plan as, in front of a crowd of 42,000 on an emotion-filled evening, with the Burnden floodlights burning brightly and illuminating all around, the home side recorded a famous and amazing 3-0 victory. A hat-trick from Gary Jones (playing alongside former Liverpool striker Roger Hunt), including a penalty, suddenly made Jimmy's team look like world beaters and even he admitted that he had no idea how. He hadn't introduced any new playing tactics or signed any major names but the team oozed confidence and seemed to be enjoying their football far more now, especially after the frustration of the previous season.

As Jimmy said in his autobiography, though, it didn't last. They only won three of their next 15 games before the end of the year, including a 6-0 home rout by Chelsea in the fourth round of the League Cup. By this time, Jimmy was having doubts. Not just about the team but doubts now about his ability to be a manager. Nothing he introduced worked and Bolton were slipping down the table. Another defeat by Chelsea in the FA Cup meant there was little to play for unless Jimmy could somehow turn things around and it was at this time that he received a visit from the chairman, Jack Banks.

Banks, as has already been described, was a straight-talking northerner. He drove a Rolls-Royce but wore clothes that would be perfect for the book and later-TV character Worzel Gummidge. He often arrived at the ground with a flask of soup, that his wife had made him, and a bottle of whisky – just in case the soup didn't warm him up sufficiently. On this occasion, he walked into Jimmy's office with the whisky and insisted Jim shared a glass with him. It looked like it was the end for the rookie manager but, instead, Banks told him in no uncertain terms that he had appointed Jimmy because he was told that the new manager would give the youth players a chance.

'Let me know when you decide to play them because they will be a damn sight better than what we've had out for the last few weeks,' he said, and with that, he left the office. It brought it home to Jimmy that he hadn't done what was promised and, in fact, he was failing at his job. His Bolton Wanderers were no better than the team that had been relegated and there were already whispers and discontent among the Burnden faithful. The local press wasn't slow to start asking questions, with some suggesting that the club had made a mistake in appointing a player who had never managed anywhere, never mind at a famous old club like Bolton. It was clear that he had to change his way of working and that's what he did.

With a new mix of younger players and a new training regime in which Jimmy encouraged what he described as 'push-and-run football', the team's fortunes started to improve. From April 1972, they played 12 games and lost only two of them, eventually finishing in a respectable eighth place, admittedly some 20 points behind champions Aston Villa but certainly better than was expected halfway through the season. It's notable that the club he turned down, Blackburn Rovers, now managed by Ken Furphy, finished one place below them.

The following season was near perfect for Jimmy and Bolton. Without making too many changes and also resisting the advances of Manchester City for the man who'd scored a hat-trick against them, Gary Jones, the team improved as each week passed. After a slow start, they then got into their stride and by January 1973 they were top of the league, where they

Working in the Blackpool Gazette offices post-playing career.

Leading the team out for the second half – Blackpool captain 1968/69 season.

Jimmy with Preston's Tom Finney. They had enormous respect for each other.

Captaining England against Scotland at Hampden Park – 11/4/64. Scotland won 1-0.

Captaining England against the Rest of the World at Wembley – the great Alfredo di Stefano opposite.

A youthful Jimmy in his favourite place – Blackpool beach.

Tracksuited and injured. A forlorn-looking Jimmy on the England sidelines.

Pre-season Blackpool FC publicity photo – 1968/69 season.

On his way to Brazil and a first international cap for England!

Despite not being in the team, Jimmy had as much pride as the rest. England are world champions!

Warming up during the 1955/56 season. Jimmy was awarded the Young Player of the Year at the end of the season.

Jimmy and his wife Anne with the trophy

A World Cup qualifier away to Portugal in May 1961

A pre-season publicity shot ahead of the 1968/69 Blackpool campaign.

Jimmy's last professional game. Home to Manchester United as Bobby Charlton shakes his hand and both teams form a guard of honour.

stayed until the end of the season. Their record of 25 victories in 46 games meant they finished at the head of the league by four points from Notts County and a further two ahead of Blackburn Rovers. The crowds had come back, with an average of around 17,500 for the season and a bumper 21,000 for the final game of the campaign against Brentford. Jimmy was a hero.

By winning the Third Division with Bolton Wanderers in 1973, he did what he was unable to do as a player and that was to win a trophy. It's not lost on the author that, despite being one of the greatest players the country has produced, Jimmy's playing trophy cabinet was bare, apart from a medal for winning promotion with Blackpool in 1970. No FA Cup medal, no World Cup medal (although that was to come years later when the FA finally agreed to let the whole squad have one) and no Anglo-Italian medal, as he had retired just weeks before Blackpool won that particular trophy. Now he had a title medal as a manager and it must have been something he was immensely proud of. This came about, not as part of a team, but mainly due to his own moulding of a bunch of players who had previously failed to gel. This was Jimmy's team and they had been successful.

It's also worth noting that this league title was only Bolton Wanderers' second in their history. They won the Second Division in the early part of the century but, for a club with such a long and illustrious history (a bit like Blackpool, to show how both clubs mirror each other), they had won little at league level.

For Jimmy, though, there was a bittersweet, if not rather painful, moment when Bolton officially became champions. It was at Port Vale in the penultimate game of the season and as

John Byrom scored the equalising goal that secured the title, Jimmy jumped up in the dugout and immediately cracked his head open on the concrete cover, nearly knocking himself out! Stitches and an aching head followed. It was probably worth it!

Jimmy had become popular with the Bolton supporters for obvious reasons but it had been a hard road to travel. Within a year of his appointment, club legend Nat Lofthouse left his position as general manager and Jimmy was blamed by many for the departure of the man who defined the club the way Stan Mortensen did at Blackpool. The facts were, though, that Bolton were in the Third Division and finances couldn't stretch to the luxury of a general manager. It seems harsh but there was little Jimmy could do about it. Thankfully, Lofthouse returned to the club a few years later in a commercial role but there are still those today who blame Jimmy Armfield for the departure of the famous 'Lion of Vienna' from Burnden Park.

Finances were stretched for Bolton's return to the Second Division when they bought Liverpool winger Peter Thompson in December 1973. It was only £15,000 (and actually Jimmy managed to persuade Bill Shankly to let him join Bolton instead of Coventry City, who had offered £50,000!) but it was a lot of money in the 1970s. Thompson became the instant star of the team, the favourite among the supporters and most of the other players. They comfortably survived in the Second Division, a campaign that saw Jimmy return to Bloomfield Road for the first time since he retired. He was given an outstanding ovation by the Blackpool fans and repaid them by winning 2-0!

Sadly, his next return, later that year at the start of the 1974/75 season, was one of the most harrowing imaginable.

The rivalry between Blackpool and Bolton Wanderers had always been friendly and respectful, until the blight of football hooliganism arrived. Blackpool, being a seaside resort, was a magnet for opposing supporters to arrive in huge numbers and, so, Bloomfield Road played host to larger crowds than expected. Along with the large attendances came the threat of violence, particularly at a ground that had virtually no segregation, with opposing supporters separated by a line of police down the entire length of the Kop.

It was in this scenario on 24 August 1974 that the first murder took place at an English football ground. Kevin Olsson, just 18 years of age, was stabbed during a melee near the toilets at the back of the Kop. He died from his injuries and it was a defining moment in the battle against hooliganism. The game continued, despite the mayhem that was taking place in the ground, and it was only later that Jimmy became aware of the seriousness of what had happened. During the match, Bolton player Alan Waldron had broken his leg and Jimmy visited him in hospital. It was, ironically, only at that point that he learned of the death of the Blackpool fan. He knew he had to do something. In an interview given much later to a local newspaper reporter, he tried to explain his feelings:

> That night I went to see the family of the boy who had been killed. Anne came with me and we parked in the street near their house. We sat in the car for a while, wondering whether or not to go in but we both knew we had to ... I was still regarded as a Blackpool man by everyone in the town, because that's what I was, but

131

I was also now representing Bolton. I had to do it. We went to the front door and knocked, not knowing what kind of reception we would get.

It was the father who opened it. I remember I said something like 'I don't know what I'm going to say to you but we thought we should come'. Obviously, he was shaken, but he recognised me and we went inside. I honestly didn't know what to say to him, except, 'Everyone at Bolton is desperately sorry and we regret what has happened'. I think I said something about not knowing what I could do, but me and Anne would always be there for the family. It was an awful time.

It was a dreadful day in the history of English football, never mind the history of both Blackpool and Bolton Wanderers, and, sadly, despite their own traditional rivalries, there are still some supporters of both clubs who refuse to let the appalling moment go. A rivalry that barely existed before that moment is now exaggerated by those who played no part in the dreadful incident. It was one of the things that always saddened Jimmy Armfield but, in the 1970s, at the birth of hooliganism, attending a football match was not always the peaceful and enjoyable afternoon's entertainment it had been in the past.

Jimmy had three years at Bolton Wanderers and had gone some way to resurrecting the fortunes of the famous old club. He'd taken them from the depths of despair following their fall into the Third Division and dragged them back into the second tier but his job was done. It had been a well-done job, too. By the time the start of the 1974/75 season approached, Bolton fans were so nervous of losing him that they actually started a petition to make him stay! There were rumours that Blackpool wanted him back and that even First Division Everton had made enquiries. He was clearly popular. Paul Jones was one of the regular defenders at the club and he had nothing but praise for his manager. In an interview with the *Bolton News*, he said:

> Jimmy was one of the kindest, most honest blokes you could ever wish to meet. He got us together, fostered that 'one for all' spirit, but I can't remember him ever getting angry. He didn't swear once the whole time I played for him and you'd never imagine that of a manager these days. He commanded respect because of what he'd done in the game. The group didn't give him many problems but if there was something to be sorted, it would be done in his office, behind closed doors, with nothing coming out into the press. What he did for Bolton at that time possibly doesn't get the recognition it should. Nat Lofthouse gave me my debut but it was Jim who really brought me and a few others on. Jimmy started what Ian Greaves finished off. Those two men together created that whole era in the late 70s where we had a bit of success and were a decent side. He was a pleasure to work for.

It was clear that Jimmy had made his name as a manager and now was the time to move to a bigger club. He had to leave the small-town mentality of a Blackpool and a Bolton and tax himself, test himself at a club where success was demanded, not just expected. There weren't too many clubs who fulfilled the criteria who were looking for a manager, except one. A club who defined the word 'success' in the 1970s but also a club that defined the word 'ruthless' in the way they conducted themselves. A club that Don Revie had moulded into the ultimate playing football family and the club that Brian Clough had effectively destroyed in a tumultuous and soap opera-driven 44 days. That club was Leeds. Leeds United. The most successful and, in some ways, the most despised club in England. That's where Jimmy was going. They asked him in October 1974, at a time when it was consumed in a maelstrom of controversy. On the fourth of that month, Jimmy bid farewell to the ramshackle Burnden Park, the cotton mills and the passion that exists in small-time northern football clubs and he said hello to Leeds United. A club of glamour. A club of big-name players and a club that had European aspirations. It was like a local councillor suddenly becoming prime minister within 24 hours. It was a huge step up but Jimmy had the confidence, the self-belief and the backing to know he'd be a success. Leeds, Leeds United!

Chapter 15:

Leeds, Leeds, Leeds ...

AH, LEEDS United. Has there ever been a club that has polarised opinion so much as Leeds United? Even back in 1974, they were on the receiving end of a love-hate relationship with football supporters. The great and mighty Leeds United were never loved. They were respected, though. As probably the biggest club in English football in the early part of the decade, they were respected.

Leeds' reputation, good and bad, was forged during the lengthy and extremely successful Don Revie era. He created a team who steamrollered the opposition and seemingly won everything in sight. Some would say that they should have won a lot more but two First Division titles plus FA Cup, League Cup and Inter-Cities Fairs Cup successes seem pretty impressive looking back down the years. A 'family' of players is what Revie created. Revie called every player by his Christian name and they were all pals together. They were unbreakable, until the temptation of the England job lured Revie away, just at a time when they were ready to conquer Europe. That flirtation with England didn't last too long, though, as a far more desirable relationship arrived and Revie burnt his bridges and effectively disappeared from English football. When he left Leeds United, he left them as First Division champions.

So, along came Brian Clough. Leeds needed a new manager and, for reasons beyond the comprehension of most, they chose the one man who seemed to dislike everything about the club. He was someone who could never have been described as the 'perfect fit' for Leeds United. The 'square peg in a round hole' phrase could have been invented for him and Leeds United. His 44-day stay at Elland Road has been chronicled so many times that there really isn't anything else to add. His introductory comment to the squad that they could 'throw all of your medals in the bin because they were not won fairly' was probably the worst motivational speech in history. He managed one win in seven games and drove the players to the verge of a mutiny. Now he was gone and Leeds needed someone else.

The Leeds board decided they needed a completely different character from the hard-nosed Don Revie or the erratic Brian Clough, so they looked at Jimmy Armfield – still manager at Bolton Wanderers – and knew he had the steady temperament, respect and experience to put the club back where it belonged – and that was at the top.

Jimmy met four of the directors at the Clifford Arms Hotel in Lytham. Manny Cousins, Bob Roberts, Sydney Simon and Sam Bolton and, as he later revealed, they didn't seem to know too much about how the club was run. It appeared that Revie had been such a powerful force that he had effectively controlled just about everything. He also said that it wasn't actually an interview. They asked him no footballing questions, didn't ask about his family or his personal life or if he was willing to relocate to the city. Nothing. They did offer him the job, though, and Jimmy, being rightly cautious, said he would consider it.

This was one of the most difficult decisions he had ever had to make. There is a feeling that, deep down, he regretted not leaving Blackpool during his playing days, as far bigger clubs approached and knocked on the door. His loyalty was admirable but it didn't bring him success in terms of trophies. He had also started to think the same was happening at Bolton. They were back in the Second Division but only the most ardent and blinkered fan would believe that they could one day challenge the likes of Arsenal, Liverpool and, of course, Leeds United at the top of the English game. He'd been there three years. Was it time to really challenge himself at what was the biggest club in the English game?

He talked it over with Anne and they both decided that if he took the job, they wouldn't relocate, forcing Duncan and John to move schools. It wasn't fair. It was something which, in later years, Duncan really appreciated and understood. No matter what his father had to do, he wouldn't disrupt the family.

Whilst mulling over his options, and probably looking for ways to convince himself that it was a good idea, he received a phone call from the one man who could persuade him – Don Revie. There is some confusion as to whether Revie was aware that Jimmy had been offered the Leeds job but Jimmy was pretty adamant that he did. After all, even though he was now the England manager, he still seemed to be sat on the shoulders of the decision-makers at Elland Road. There was no way he would not be aware. With that in mind, Jimmy and Anne travelled to London.

Revie actually offered Jimmy the England Under-23 coach's job but it was politely declined for obvious reasons. When it was pointed out to Revie that the Leeds manager's job had been offered, he didn't flinch or seem surprised. Instead, he advised Jimmy to take it without hesitation. That was enough and within hours Jimmy had resigned from Bolton Wanderers and accepted the Leeds United position, probably the biggest domestic job in English football and certainly the one with the highest profile.

Elland Road can be seen from the motorway as you approach the city of Leeds. Even 50 years ago, the ground looked impressive and cried out 'success' to all those who saw it. On Saturday, 5 October 1974, the spectre of the ground looming over its surroundings must have felt intimidating. Certainly, the reception Jimmy received from the players at a pre-match meal in Roundhay was underwhelming as they nodded quietly to him and averted their eyes. Billy Bremner, Peter Lorimer, Johnny Giles, Allan Clarke and Terry Yorath were part of a team that, despite winning their previous home game 5-1, were making a rather weak and spineless defence of their league title. This was the first time they had met their new manager and none of them seemed particularly excited about it. The game against Arsenal that afternoon was a big test, especially as they had been managerless for a month. Jimmy said little to the players except this:

What the hell are you doing near the bottom of the league? I've played against you, I've watched you play many times and I know how good you can be. You won the title only a few months ago. So, what the hell's going on?

Maybe a little too confrontational but there was little reaction. Jimmy drove to Elland Road and made his way through the army of photographers and journalists to take his seat in the directors' box. It was bedlam. There had even been a television crew outside the family home in Blackpool recording his every move. At Leeds, the attention became overwhelming and he needed security to safely guide him into the ground, where he could locate his office before watching the game, his reactions of more interest to some photographers than what was happening on the pitch! Thankfully, Leeds won 2-0 and Jimmy tried to look composed throughout, smoking his favourite pipe as the two points were gratefully collected. The sight of a football manager smoking a pipe at a football match is now at odds with the game but in 1974 it was perfectly natural and acceptable. It also calmed Jimmy's nerves as he considered the magnitude of the task ahead. Leeds had won but it wasn't very impressive.

One of the first things he had to do was appoint a physio! Amazingly, the all-powerful Leeds United relied on their kitman to treat injuries, which meant he was either incredibly talented and wasted in his main job or the club were extremely lucky with serious injuries. At least they had a club secretary but there did seem to be a chasm of difference between how Bolton and Leeds were set up – and not the way one would have expected.

There was little respite, as they then had two more home games in the next five days. That was typically 1970s football, an age when just about everything cried out 'excess', but on the Monday they beat Huddersfield Town 2-1 in a League Cup second round replay and then, two days later, they beat Bury by the same scoreline in the third round! Jimmy hadn't been in the job for seven days, yet he'd overseen three victories. It was hardly surprising the local press were over-hyping the 'saviour' of Leeds United.

Within a fortnight, Jimmy had his first taste of European action as either a player or a manager. It's incredible to think that he had never played in a European fixture with Blackpool – missing the brief Anglo-Italian tournament, as he had retired a couple of weeks earlier – and Bolton had never been in that position. Now, he was on the way to Hungary to take on Újpest Dozsa in the European Cup second round. From trips to Blackburn, Millwall and Port Vale, to the glamour of a European night in a foreign country, it was a whirlwind start to top-level management.

European football in the 1970s seemed to be all about Ajax and strange-sounding names of clubs in lands that few knew about. Even Ajax was pronounced like the washing powder until the sophistication of the 1980s arrived. Europe wasn't a cheap flight away or a ferry ride to the nearest duty-free warehouse. Europe was an expensive holiday destination, mostly in Spain. Hungary was a place that you had to squint at on a map and try to pronounce it correctly. They played football and once upon a time they had played it very well, but now to what level? Even Jimmy wasn't sure. As it was, they played it well but not as well as the English champions. In front of a passionate and intimidating crowd, Peter Lorimer gave Leeds an early lead with an incredible volley, only for Duncan McKenzie to be sent off after 14 minutes. An equaliser was followed by a Gordon McQueen goal and Leeds held on for a well-deserved victory. The second leg was a more comfortable 3-0 win. The league form was patchy, though, and by the end of the year, Jimmy had seen eight victories but five defeats. The team were still struggling. So, in that 'what do we do now?' type moment, Jimmy came up with the most unusual of solutions.

Chapter 16:

Leeds WILL go to the ball

IN 1974, Leeds United were probably the most famous collection of individuals in the country. The Beatles had long gone, The Rolling Stones and The Who were intermittent at best and few sports seemed to be able to tap into the new craze for celebrity. Only football, despite its myriad of terrace problems, seemed to offer a solution but, with the England team in disgrace after failing to qualify for the World Cup and Manchester United languishing in the Second Division, it was now down to Leeds United to bring the glamour to football.

The team weren't loved but they were known. Allan 'Sniffer' Clarke, Norman 'Bite Yer legs' Hunter, Peter 'Hotshot' Lorimer and 'Little' Billy Bremner, all strutting around the pitch with their unique sock tabs that made the all-white kit look incredibly trendy. They played out their dramas on the television more times than any other team, so they had all become household names, but by December 1974, they were still uncomfortably close to the relegation zone. Somehow, Jimmy had to find a way to re-bond the players and get back the famous team spirit inspired by Don Revie and dismantled by Brian Clough. A trip to Spain for a week's sunbathing? A night out with wives and girlfriends at the theatre? Maybe a party for all the families at the ground? No, none of these. Instead, and for reasons that even to this day aren't really clear, Jimmy decided to get his players to act in a Christmas pantomime.

It wasn't quite that straightforward, though. Jimmy had become friends with Barney Colehan. He was a Leeds United supporter but also a showbiz impresario and the man who ran the City Varieties Music Hall in Leeds. As well as that, he was responsible for the successful TV show *The Good Old Days* and had played a part in a pre-FA Cup Final version of *It's a Knockout* in 1972 involving the finalists, Leeds United and Arsenal. Jimmy had started talking about putting on a fancy dress party at Christmas for the players and their families but somehow this evolved into a pantomime that Jimmy would present and script, with Colehan happy to put it on at his theatre. It helped that it was Paul Reaney's testimonial year, so the proceeds would go to that and to charitable causes. It seemed a crazy idea, yet it worked. How he managed to convince the players that this was a good idea is an achievement in itself. From his recollections, it seemed that the only player who was enthused was Duncan McKenzie. As he was still struggling to be accepted in a Revie-dominated squad, this was a great way of using his natural temperament to become part of the group. The likes of Bremner and Hunter took a little more persuading, but persuaded they were and Jimmy added to their daily training routine by getting them to learn the lines he had written for each character of *Cinderella*, the name of this crazy pantomime idea.

The pantomime was a 60-minute amusing and in-joke affair, with cheesy lines like 'here's Cinders coming from the Forest' in relation to McKenzie's move from the Nottingham club and his new role as the lead character. All the players were given full costumes and their own five-minutes-of-fame lines to say. The theatre, which was famous enough to have boasted appearances by Charlie Chaplin and Harry Houdini in years past, was packed to capacity, with the audience even standing in the aisles, and they loved every minute of the performance, clapping and cheering so much that the 60 minutes became 90.

For those with a vivid imagination, a knowledge of the players involved and the open-mindedness to accept that this actually happened, then they will see in their mind's eye McKenzie dressed as Cinderella, Billy Bremner as Buttons, strolling down the centre of the theatre smoking and throwing sweets to the children, Gordon McQueen as the Good Fairy, Paul Reaney as Prince Charming and Jimmy himself as the Master of Ceremonies. The performance only lasted for two nights – due to the rather irritating intervention of a football game – but it seemed to work. Leeds only lost three of their last 17 league matches and finished closer to champions Derby County than the relegation zone. They progressed to the quarter-finals of the FA Cup, where it took Ipswich Town *four* games to knock them out and, of course, there was Europe. The European adventure really started after the turn of the year. It became the one thing that defined Jimmy's time as the Leeds United manager and was all inspired by a bunch of footballers dressed in drag on stage. One can only imagine what the likes of Sir Alex Ferguson or Arsène Wenger might have made of it.

Leeds played Belgian champions Anderlecht in the European Cup quarter-finals, overwhelming them 3-0 at Elland Road, with Jordan, McQueen and Lorimer scoring, before a Bremner-inspired 1-0 win in the second leg. It had been an intimidating atmosphere but Jimmy had got the team playing well and now they faced the might of Barcelona, including Johan Cruyff and Johan Neeskens. On a crazy night in April and in front of 50,000 fans at Elland Road, where the bright floodlights could almost illuminate the tension, Leeds beat them 2-1 with goals from Bremner and Clarke. The feeling was that the second leg would be far tougher, especially with more than 100,000 fans expected to be at the Camp Nou. Barcelona, one of the world's biggest and most famous clubs, roared on by a passionate Catalan crowd who felt it was their divine right to enjoy footballing success. There could not have been a tougher test.

It proved to be one of the greatest nights in Jimmy Armfield's career, either as a player or a manager, and showed that his reading of a game had matured and progressed to the extent that he could comfortably stand toe-to-toe with the greats. In the opposite dugout was one of the world's greatest coaches, Rinus Michels, a man who was certainly not used to losing. Although this was effectively a Don Revie team that was ready to take on the best of Europe, it had now been sprinkled with a little bit of Armfield fairydust (obviously, the pantomime connection was still there) and, on the night, tactical changes during the game and the reaction to a harsh sending-off proved that Jimmy had become the all-round football manager. This was the night that, under Jimmy, Leeds United suddenly became the great European team that everyone had predicted they would be.

Jimmy had earned a reputation for being indecisive as a manager and he was actually often ridiculed with the phrase 'his indecision is final', which was something that followed him even after he retired from football management. He was an easy target, as mild-mannered Jimmy Armfield certainly wouldn't react publicly to such a slur, and it was an inaccurate accusation, too. To prove how words can be damaging, the case for his defence can rest with the strong decision he made ahead of the return leg when he replaced the ever-reliable Paul Reaney in defence with Trevor Cherry, believing he would be the more positive player on the night. He also instructed Peter Lorimer to start on the left and then switch to the right after ten minutes in the hope of confusing the Barcelona defence. It seemed to work, as Leeds started off the evening as the stronger team.

The stadium in Barcelona is an impressive sight and even the roofless 1975 version held enough noise to make it difficult to think, never mind try to convey instructions from the touchline. There was a small band of Leeds supporters who had made their way to the Basque region at a time when cheap flights were still to be introduced to the nation's psyche, so the Leeds players had around 100,000 screaming Barcelona supporters to contend with – and what a noise they made.

That noise was silenced in the first half when Lorimer volleyed into the net to give Leeds a two-goal aggregate advantage but, like the wounded animal that keeps on fighting, Barcelona just produced wave after wave of attacks, finally getting their reward with around 20 minutes left. That was followed by an inexplicable sending-off for McQueen, who was involved in an altercation with another player. It not only put Leeds down to ten men but it meant he would miss the final should they get there. As he disconsolately walked back to the dressing room, Jimmy showed his caring side, effectively ignoring the rule book by which managers are supposed to behave. He went to the dressing room to console the Scottish centre-back. Jimmy was later to explain in a BBC Radio Leeds interview why he did it:

> I always try to console a player if he is injured or sent off during a game. I do that because I've been in that situation when I've suffered an injury and sat in the room listening to the crowd outside. I was never sent off in my career but I suffered my share of injuries and knew from experience that a dressing room can be one of the loneliest places when you have to leave the game for any reason ... Gordon, bless him, was in tears. He realised that if we went on to reach the final, he wouldn't be playing. I could only imagine the pain he was suffering.

Leeds hung on to win 3-2 on aggregate. They were in the European Cup Final, the first English team to make it since the victorious Manchester United side that beat Benfica 4-1 at Wembley in 1968. They would play the West German giants, Bayern Munich, in Paris. It was the dream that everyone connected to the club had aspired to throughout the Revie era and one could only imagine what was going through the former manager's mind that evening. It is said that he attended the game in Barcelona but didn't make himself known to the players or Jimmy. It would have been a bittersweet moment. As it was, Jimmy Armfield's Leeds United had made it to the biggest club game in Europe.

Chapter 17:

A night to remember ...
A night to forget

THE EUROPEAN Cup Final of 1975 is still one of the most talked about in the history of the competition but, sadly, for the wrong reasons. It was played at the Parc des Princes in Paris and Leeds' opponents were the holders, Bayern Munich. The German side had had a pretty disastrous domestic campaign and had finished in mid-table. It meant they had to win the game to qualify for the following season's European Cup. The build-up to the final was intense and this was one of the biggest tests for Jimmy Armfield as a manager. This was still, in effect, a Don Revie team and that team had also under-produced by only finishing in ninth place in their defence of the First Division title. That blame was laid primarily at the departed Brian Clough's door but some of the fans had their misgivings about Jimmy. So, winning the biggest prize in European football might just go some way to winning them over completely.

The final was to be held exactly a month after the last game of the domestic season in England. That meant a busy period arranging friendly fixtures to keep the players fit and finely tuned. Matches against a Norwegian side, a testimonial against a Don Revie XI of all things, a friendly with Walsall and another against a Scottish under-23 team kept the momentum going. It certainly seems rather haphazard today but that was football in the 1970s.

The team didn't actually travel to Paris until the day before the game, by which time the cultural capital of love and romance was playing host to a Yorkshire invasion. How the French and the refined people of Leeds managed to communicate is one of those eternal mysteries but the days leading up to the game were peaceful and fun-filled.

As Jimmy had introduced a pantomime atmosphere to the club a few months previously, it was fitting that the Parc des Princes should see its own pantomime villain in French referee Michel Kitabdjian. His performance that evening was so catastrophically inept, with some of the worst decisions seen at a major final, that even Jimmy was heard to say to his assistant, Bob English, that he hoped the game would end 0-0, as the only way they would win the cup would be with a replay.

Maybe it started after a truly horrific tackle in the fourth minute by Terry Yorath that saw Bayern's Bjorn Andersson stretchered off but the referee then appeared to do everything in his power to deny Leeds victory. They were dominant but a clear handball by Franz Beckenbauer in the first half was waved away, as was a challenge on Allan Clarke by the captain in the penalty area, which even Beckenbauer later admitted was a definite penalty. It got worse. That seemed unlikely but it did.

A perfectly good goal by Peter Lorimer in the 66th minute was disallowed for an offside infringement by Billy Bremner.

The problem was, the referee had already turned back to the centre circle and the linesman was at the halfway line. A few words from the German players, notably Beckenbauer, persuaded the now-panic stricken referee to disallow it. Obviously, Bayern scored twice and the dreams of the Leeds players and supporters were evaporating into the smoke-bombed air of Paris. The Leeds United supporters, never known for their sporting reaction to defeat, caused havoc, ripping up seats and clashing with riot police. The trouble inside the stadium resulted in a German TV operator losing an eye, another suffering a broken arm and around £50,000 worth of damage being caused to technical equipment. The violence continued through the night on the streets of Paris, leading to a four-year European ban for the club. The referee, given a poor mark by the UEFA officials present at the final, was castigated by all. There was hardly a single word of praise.

Jimmy took it badly yet, at his post-match conference, he was the calm and reassuring man that everyone knew and loved. In typical understatement he said:

> I did not agree with his decisions but that's football. I thought the decisions hurt our team. If anything, we had too much of the ball. We did all the running and tired ourselves out. The lads played well. They played their hearts out and I think that makes it worse.

As the years passed, though, his words became harsher. It could be the knowledge in hindsight that it was his last real opportunity at winning a major trophy but whenever the game was mentioned to him, his response was always that it had been a scandal and that the referee was the worst he had ever seen. Whatever had caused such a truly awful performance by the referee was never established. There certainly didn't appear to be any impropriety involved. It was just one of those nights where it seemed he made more bad decisions than good. The problem was, he made them in the biggest football game in Europe.

The injustice of the evening carried on beyond just the 90 minutes of the final. The four-year ban seemed unnecessarily harsh and Jimmy decided he would fight UEFA and try and get it either overturned or, at worst, reduced. He did this without a single member of the Leeds United board of directors showing any interest in offering any help. Twice he travelled to the UEFA headquarters in Geneva, only accompanied by a newspaper journalist on each occasion. The first time he was gently reprimanded for not compiling a sufficient defence, so he returned to his home in Blackpool and prepared again. He returned for a second time. He paid his own expenses, flights and hotel and, after producing a document outlining the complaints from the supporters about heavy-handed French police tactics, the ban was reduced to two years. Effectively, it didn't matter, as Leeds didn't get anywhere near European qualification for many years, but Jimmy had been successful. Sadly, that was neither acknowledged nor appreciated by the board of directors but they did at least reimburse his travelling costs. Jimmy had gone beyond the call of the manager's duty book but he may as well have not bothered.

Chapter 18:

Goodbye to the family

IN LATER years, many of the players said that they felt the loss in the European Cup Final was the worst possible thing that could have happened to the club. If they had won, then the club's profile would have been huge all around the world and they would have been able to attract the top players to not only continue the domination they had shown domestically, but also at a higher level. Obviously, that didn't happen and Jimmy Armfield was now left with the task of breaking up the ageing 'family' from the Revie era.

It wasn't easy and this was also felt by Jimmy's own sons, Duncan and John. They had reached an age now where they were aware of their father's profession and had got used to wandering around the dressing room at Elland Road or attending parties where Billy Bremner, Johnny Giles, Norman Hunter and Allan Clarke and others were present. As Duncan said: 'We knew them all, and they were like friends, really. It never occurred to me that we were fortunate or special because we saw these people regularly. It was just Dad's job.'

Dad's job, though, had taken on a more ruthless role and the Revie squad that he had inherited was slowly dismantled. It wasn't a case of stamping his authority on a club that had relied on Don Revie for so long that it sometimes wondered how it could function without him, but more to do with the age of the players. They were still effective but they were no longer winners. Leeds United had built up a winning mentality but these players were now being left behind. They were being moved on methodically and, in some ways, almost brutally. It was done with the care and gentleness that came with Jimmy's personality but it was done in a ruthless fashion, nonetheless. The 'manager's indecision is final' really no longer applied. It wasn't something he enjoyed at all, as he still had memories of having to tell young players at Bolton Wanderers that they were to be released due to the financial realities of a club that could never compete at the top table. It hurt him then and it hurt him now, especially as these players had lived, breathed and dreamed of Leeds United. It was difficult, too, to convince the supporters who had become so close to those in the famous white shirts.

The next season, 1975/76, Leeds finished fifth, quite a respectable position and only just short of a UEFA Cup spot they would not have been allowed to take up, but the personnel was changing. Billy Bremner, Johnny Giles, Norman Hunter, Allan Clarke, Paul Reaney, Terry Cooper, Terry Yorath, Mick Bates and, even though he was the top scorer at the time, Duncan McKenzie, all left Leeds over the next couple of years. It was a seismic shock but they were replaced. Tony Currie was a big-name signing from Sheffield United, Paul Hart joined from Blackpool (who had been relegated to the Third Division for the first time in their history) and Brian Flynn arrived from Burnley but it was clear that the squad was not of the standard collectively as the 'Revie family'. Despite all of that, Jimmy was proud that he'd actually managed to make a profit for the club, especially as both Gordon McQueen and Joe Jordan left for Manchester United in lucrative deals. Over a three-year period, he turned a £400,000 deficit into a £250,000 profit. The problem was, Leeds were underachieving on the pitch. Reflecting on the period, Jimmy said:

> Well, I could never understand why Don Revie left when he did. He had the chance to take the side into the European Cup but he chose England instead. After that season, of course, I had to break up that side. Maybe that's what Don didn't want to do. No one can call me indecisive. Think of the players who left in my time: Terry Cooper, Norman Hunter, Gordon McQueen, Paul Reaney, Billy Bremner, Johnny Giles, Terry Yorath, Mick Bates, Joe Jordan … It's not easy getting rid of players like that. But the players I brought in did well: Tony Currie, Ray Hankin, Brian Flynn and Arthur Graham.

In the 1976/77 season, Leeds finished a distant tenth but did reach the FA Cup semi-finals, only to lose 2-1 to Manchester United. Worryingly, a crowd of just 16,891 turned up at Elland Road for the draw with West Ham United in April – the lowest since the club had returned to the First Division. The fans had become disillusioned, now starved of the success they once took for granted. Jimmy was under pressure, and he knew it, yet he kept his counsel and continued the rebuilding process.

He never felt he wasn't being supported by the board and, in particular, Manny Cussins, and had now decided that he would look for a family home in Leeds. Duncan and John were now old enough to start to make their own way in life and the travelling was becoming a burden for Jimmy. That was how secure Jimmy felt whilst manager at Leeds United. He did need a good season, though, and, with the likes of Ray Hankin, Currie, Clarke and Flynn, he felt he had a side strong enough to compete for the First Division title. Sadly, they never got close.

They finished ninth and reached the semi finals of the League Cup, where they were overwhelmed in two games by Brian Clough's Nottingham Forest in a predictable twist of irony. Only one win in their final seven league games meant that a return to European competition was just a dream and nowhere near becoming a reality. The local media now turned against Jimmy, with suggestions the board had lost patience with him. The sacking was, sadly, inevitable.

Like all high-profile football dismissals, it was played out in the most prolonged and publicly painful way, never giving a thought to the stress and the hurt that was being inflicted on the poor victim. Jimmy had been given an inkling that all was not well when a 'friendly' local reporter from the national Sunday newspaper *The People* came in for a chat. It seemed that the paper was going to run a story the following weekend that Jimmy was on the way out of the hotseat at Elland Road, although he wouldn't disclose his sources. This had come as news to Jimmy and one can only imagine the concern he had when he attended a board meeting at the end of the season – especially as his long-time ally, Manny Cussins, wasn't present and Bob Roberts was in the chair.

As it was, Jimmy survived the meeting and spent most of it discussing the recent tour of Switzerland where, as a 'warm down' from the campaign, they'd enjoyed comfortable victories over Etoile Carouge and Young Boys of Berne. They had then travelled to Marbella for a few days of golfing before allowing the players to take the summer weeks off. After the meeting ended, Jimmy was shocked then to be confronted by waiting reporters at reception asking if he'd been sacked! It was brutal. It was unpleasant but it was football. Still, he remained the manager of Leeds United, no matter what was being reported. All he could do was carry on and continue to prepare for the following season. That meant signing John Hawley from Hull City, who later told the tale of how he'd been signed for one of the biggest clubs in the country, only for the manager to be sacked when he informed the board! It wasn't quite true but it made for a good story.

The reality was that Jimmy went into a June board meeting that this time was being chaired by Cussins. He felt secure, as the rumour mill had quietened when nothing transpired from the regular 'Armfield to be sacked' stories and he had even arranged a holiday for two weeks immediately after the meeting. Added to that, he and Anne had seen a nice house in Harewood that they were keen on buying (from Manny Cussins, actually, as he was building a new estate there), so everything felt good. It didn't last.

Jimmy later said that he knew things weren't going to go well from the moment he walked into the boardroom. The board members looked furtive and some refused to look him in the eye. There was a tenseness and this probably wasn't helped when Jimmy's opening salvo was to ask for a new contract. To be fair to him, his existing one ended in three months' time and he had to start to plan his future for his family, hence the desire to move to the Leeds area. He didn't get the response, or the backing, that he wanted. Cussins, normally a close ally of Jimmy's, basically replied that he could wait until the end of October to see where the team were in the league. That wouldn't help Jimmy at all and, after a few terse exchanges, they adjourned.

Outside the boardroom, Manny and Jimmy spoke quietly and it was then that Cussins told him that the board had no intention of giving Jimmy a new contract under the current circumstances. He had lost the backing of the board and they were keen on bringing in someone else. When they returned to the meeting, Rayner Barker, one of the club's board members, asked Jimmy outright if he was willing to 'fight for his job', an extraordinary question which made it clear the board wanted to put Jimmy on trial for the first three months of the season and if he failed, they would sack him. That would be intolerable in any career situation but in the high-profile sport of football, it was suicide by trial. Jimmy declined and that was that. Another of the board members, Bob Roberts, confirmed they would pay Jimmy what he was due for the remainder of his contract and add £5,000 into his pension but it was harsh and it was brutal. After just under three years and four seasons, Leeds

United sacked Jimmy Armfield. At least they agreed to keep the news secret from the press until Jimmy had finished his two-week holiday but the hurt was hard and it affected him in a far greater way than even he could have imagined. Under Jimmy, Leeds had always finished in the top ten of the First Division and had also reached the semi-finals of the two domestic cup competitions but it wasn't enough. Jimmy was now out of work.

Chapter 19:

Life-changing

MOST PEOPLE reach a point in their lives when they ask the same question. What do I do now? When you've lived a life that has become comfortable and reliable and then it is torn away from you in ruthless and unsympathetic fashion, you take a step backwards and reflect.

This is what Jimmy had to do. It wasn't that no one wanted him after he was sacked by Leeds United – far from it. Leicester City, Newcastle United, Chelsea, Blackburn Rovers, for the second time, Hearts, Athletic Bilbao and even the Iranian national team had enquired after his services (the last was certainly unusual and one can only imagine how 'Gentleman Jim' would have dealt with the culture in the Shah-era or, indeed, the years that followed) but he'd lost interest. He did help out at Blackburn, though, as they were looking for a new manager and asked his advice after he turned down the position. He was able to bring in a young Howard Kendall from Stoke City but it was clear that once he had been installed in the manager's chair, Jimmy was one too many, so he departed.

It felt like he was wanted and yet, at the same time, he wasn't. In later years, he admitted to the extent of the hurt he felt after being sacked by one of the biggest clubs in the country. The fact that it had been played out in such a public and almost humiliating way also affected him. For a man who had spent his whole life treating people in the correct way – a result of his upbringing and his deep faith – to be dismissed without so much as a second thought, was more than just a blow to his pride, it was a wake-up call to himself to remember that the sport of football was becoming harsher, more ruthless and less enjoyable. He needed to find something else to do.

With hindsight, it seems a shame that Jimmy turned his back on football management. By the time he was sacked, he had become established and was regarded as a very good manager. Who knows how far he could have gone? Certainly, the top clubs were showing interest. Maybe the England job would become available? After all, once Don Revie had departed into a haze of financial whispers and promises, it was open betting on who would take, and keep, the biggest job in English football. England were on their knees after failing to qualify for two successive World Cups and, although it was too late for 1978, the next in 1982 was up for grabs, not to mention the 1980 European Championship. It's possible that Jimmy could have been a candidate but his decision to never take a footballing management job again deprived us of that footballing fantasy. Ron Greenwood's tenure from 1977 to 1982 was hardly a remarkable success, so, in that alternate universe that we sometimes live in, if Jimmy had not taken the Leeds United job and joined Don Revie as England Under-23 manager, then he probably would have become manager of the senior national team. All part of the mind's imagination but it's fun to consider how it might have turned out and how much England would have benefited.

Instead, Jimmy returned to the career that he had considered when he was still playing. The 'safety net' should things go wrong. He returned to the world of journalism, picking up where he had left off back in 1971 but determined again to start at the bottom and learn everything he needed to know to become a respected journalist. It was an immense task and one that is certainly worth reflecting on.

Jimmy Armfield was still one of the most famous names in English football. He could walk into any newspaper office or television studio and offer his services and make a living out of his opinions and his fame. That would be easy but Jimmy Armfield wasn't that type of man. He wanted to do it well and the only way was to learn from the best until he, too, could be described as one of the best.

It all restarted in one of those ways that only fate can provide. Granada Television producer Paul Doherty contacted Jimmy to see if he would be willing to contribute to the weekly *Kick Off* football programme that was broadcast in the North West of England every Sunday. The reference to fate here is that Paul was the son of former Northern Ireland international Peter Doherty, one of the finest players in Britain before the Second World War and, of course, a former Blackpool player. It may be tenuous but the connection works. Jimmy agreed.

That should have been the 'happy ever after' moment but it wasn't. Jimmy didn't appear to enjoy it that much. He wasn't initially comfortable on TV and, as he said: 'I found myself turning up on a Friday, churning out a few scripts, picking up the cheque and going home. I was in the squad but felt like a substitute – and I've never been a substitute in my life.'

Thankfully, he got a break when he met up with the northern sports editor of the *Daily Express*, Mike Dempsey. He invited Jimmy to lunch and, over coffee and sandwiches, offered him a part-time position where he could write a regular column and cover a game each weekend. It was perfect, as the newspaper's offices were in Ancoats in Greater Manchester, and it also meant that Jimmy could continue to attend games for a reason, as opposed to just turning up and accepting the inevitable hospitality. His first task, though, was to make sense of the numerous reports that arrived from the correspondents from around the north of England – Merseyside, Lancashire, Yorkshire – and turn them into a ten-paragraph article after fact-checking with managers and clubs. It was basic work but perfect for honing the discipline needed to write good, and quick, newspaper copy.

He did get the chance to go to local matches, firstly Stockport County and Tranmere Rovers, both of whom played on a Friday evening. That was followed by covering games at Bury and Preston, Blackburn and Burnley, Huddersfield and Barnsley, but very, very rarely at Blackpool or Bolton. It was probably due to the fact that it may have been awkward for Jimmy at the time but games at Bloomfield Road and Burnden Park were normally reported on by others.

Jimmy regarded Mike Dempsey highly. He was the man who taught him how to be a national newspaper journalist and he would probably have put him alongside Stanley Matthews,

Joe Smith, Alf Ramsey as the men who moulded him. Add them to his father, too, and it was clear that Jimmy Armfield was always learning. Never too old or too experienced to listen to others, it was one of his greatest traits as a human being. Having said that, he didn't listen to me when I suggested a quicker route to Charleroi in Belgium at the Euro 2000 tournament. We took his route that afternoon and got lost!

Eventually, Jimmy reached what could be regarded as the top level in regional sports reporting at a national newspaper when he was regularly asked to cover games involving Liverpool and Everton and Manchester United and City.

The important thing here is that he wasn't seen as a former footballer or manager who was filling in his time whilst waiting for a big job to come along. He was now seen as a committed journalist who asked the right questions and stood in the pouring rain after a game waiting to ask those right questions. As his radio producer, I watched as he sometimes took over my duties, picked up the microphone and went straight to Alex Ferguson or Walter Smith or David O'Leary and asked the kind of straightforward questions that I could make up in my mind but failed to deliver in the stress of the moment. He learned all of that in the time he spent at the *Daily Express*.

Sadly, the northern office of the newspaper closed in 1991 and Jimmy was never going to relocate his family at that late stage down to London, so his time there ended. He had made his mark, though. These are the words of reporter Matthew Dunn:

One of football's true gentlemen, Jimmy played 627 times for his only club Blackpool and 43 times for

England, 15 of those as captain. Then, after eight years in management split between Bolton and Leeds, he began to keep in touch with the sport he loved from the press box and make his way over to the other side of the fence.

Jimmy served as a journalist with the *Daily Express* form 1979 until 1991, with the BBC quickly identifying his clarity of thought and elegance of communication as the perfect qualities for a match summariser, a role in which he excelled for more than three decades.

His remarkable insight was no accident, however. Born in Denton, just outside Manchester, on September 21, 1935, Jimmy always expected to work for his living and was quite prepared to rough it with the rest of the press pack.

Sometimes, though, he did feel the need to put himself forward. Former Manchester United manager Ron Atkinson was getting tough at a press conference towards the end of another disappointing season in 1986 and snapped 'What do you know about the game? What have you all done?' Jimmy retorted 'Between us, we've won 43 caps, made over 600 appearances and gone to two World Cups'. Atkinson was duly humbled and that was the point.

It was my privilege to travel to Europe with Jimmy following Leeds while they lived the dream. We'd often chat at the back of the coach as the journalists were herded from airport to press conference to match. My abiding memory is how embarrassing it was that he genuinely sought out my opinion when all I wanted to do was listen to what he had to say.

Certainly, he was not trying to belittle Atkinson that afternoon. Pushing his own achievements was never Jimmy's style.

Relevant though it could have been to Leeds' Champions League run of 2000/01, Jimmy never, for instance, mentioned that his brief managerial career had included managing the side to a European Cup Final himself.

Nor that he had been declared the best right-back in the world by his peers at the 1962 World Cup – although undoubtedly his most treasured performance was on the Wurlitzer organ at Blackpool Tower as part of 80th birthday celebrations among friends and family that had been filled with vitality.

A stone's throw away from the tower, outside Bloomfield Road, stands a statue of him commissioned in 2011. It is an acknowledgement which Jimmy always appreciated deeply, even if the 'larger than life' nature of the 9ft bronze made him feel a little awkward.

Twice, he was given the role of overseeing the appointment of the next England manager, nearly 20 years after his last direct involvement with the game. But then the world's first overlapping full-back was always as relevant as he was trusted. And loved.

It's extraordinary that Jimmy managed to become as successful as a newspaper journalist as he was a footballer and manager. It was like the roles were interchangeable for him. He just seamlessly moved from one to the other and that was before he moved into radio broadcasting! His written word was eloquent, not a single one wasted and, after years of training he was able to convey his feelings and his opinions with the minimum number of words. That well-known phrase 'why use five words when 500 will do', which can be easily attached to some of the commentators and pundits today, was never further from his way of working. When you spoke to him personally, it was the same. He would respond in a gentle and calm way, making sure that everything he said resonated and meant something to the person he was speaking to. That came through in his columns for the newspaper and in his later role as one of the BBC's greatest-ever analysts and pundits. Only when you sat next to him and saw how he dealt with the firebrand of a football commentator – you felt the gentleness of his reasoned comments compared to what had gone before – did you understand the depth and the breadth of the knowledge that Jimmy had of the sport he loved.

During all of this, he remained loyal to the town of Blackpool and, of course, to his beloved family of Anne, Duncan and John. It's probably a fair comment to say that he was 'grounded' by them and, so, he was never seduced by the adulation and respect he received on the pitch or in the dugout or in the press box. Every day, when he could, he would return to his family home. One of the reasons why he rarely ventured south of Birmingham in later years when he was working was because he wanted to be able to get home on a Saturday evening, which meant he would be able to play the church organ on a Sunday morning. Family came first and foremost.

For an older generation, Jimmy Armfield was one of the greatest full-backs the English game had produced. A later generation saw him as a successful manager and a much younger generation read his words every week. Now there was a new generation who were about to charmed and entertained by the voice that was perfect for radio. Jimmy went from player to manager to journalist to radio personality, the way Monday becomes Tuesday, which becomes Wednesday and then Thursday. When most people are looking at retirement, he was reinventing himself and making new memories as a radio man. Add that to his FA role, of which we will come to soon, and Jimmy was as busy as ever. Again, as an example as to how much he was admired at this stage of his life, here's an excerpt from an article written by David Walker of the *Daily Mirror*.

If Jimmy called Old Trafford asking for Alex Ferguson, he usually got his man. He appreciated the problems emerging from the press box as a generation of journalists he'd grown up with moved on into retirement. But he always retained his sharp sense of humour and willingness to poke fun.

Jimmy was a habitual cap wearer and would earnestly tell the Young Turks around him how they'd be losing 30 per cent of their body heat through their heads on a cold matchday. On one occasion, a young journo spotted Jim's patchwork quilt cap and taunted him with 'what's that you've got on your head Jimmy'?

Quick as a flash Jimmy retorted 'If you don't like this one, I've got 42 others at home. Those were, of course, his England caps.

As I prepared to rake over the embers of the previous day's woes, Jimmy calmly interjected and said 'You know I had real problems this morning. There was something wrong with the stops on the church organ. We'll have to get it sorted out.'

Chapter 20:

Turn the radio on

IT'S EASY to think that Jimmy moved from newspaper reporting to radio reporting as a natural forwards step, but it didn't quite work out that way. When he was still the manager at Leeds United, he'd built up a working relationship with John Helm, who worked at BBC Radio Leeds. At that time, Helm asked Jimmy if he would be willing to partake in a short radio series where he would interview some of the Yorkshire personalities of the time, something Jimmy did exceptionally well. These weren't footballers or, indeed, just sporting stars, they were from all areas of life. Yes, there was the legendary Yorkshire cricketer Ray Illingworth, but there was also the miners' leader Arthur Scargill, actor James Fox and the Archbishop of York! Each one was treated to the charm of Jimmy as he asked the questions and it was this introduction to radio which showed him that the spoken word was so important. As we are all told when we first start working for the medium, it's a chance to paint a picture. Take the listener to a place in their mind's eye by describing the surrounding environment. With Jimmy's careful choice of wording and his deliberate delivery, he was the perfect voice for radio – even if he used to joke that he was the perfect face, too!

It was shortly after he left Elland Road, and whilst still working for the *Daily Express*, that Jimmy was introduced to the role that millions of younger football fans only remember him for, that of a radio summariser. Helm had moved to BBC Manchester and was in charge of the sports output – predominantly football – on a Saturday and he was looking for new faces (or new voices, to be exact), so asked if Jimmy would be the summariser at Maine Road the following weekend for a Manchester City game. Jimmy said yes and that's how it started.

Those early days on BBC Radio 2 alongside the incredible talents of Peter Jones and Bryon Butler, to name but two, were a huge learning curve for Jimmy. He could speak well, he knew all about football, but he had to learn to speak well and impart his knowledge of the game in a disciplined way. If he was reporting at a game, there had to be a maximum of 40 seconds to tell its story. If he was a summariser, he had to complement the commentator, who had just explained *what* had happened. Jimmy had to explain *why* it had happened. Jimmy's knowledge of the history of football was invaluable, too, as he could remind listeners of previous games he had either played in or had seen. His experience was irreplaceable and it is worth mentioning that his long-standing service to BBC Radio – on Radio 2, Radio 5 and then Radio 5 Live – was unmatched by anyone else. Whilst the trends in football came and went, there was one constant and that was Jimmy Armfield.

I witnessed this on many occasions when I was his producer at the BBC. He was respected by everyone, whether it be the press or managers or the players. There were some younger players who had probably never heard of his football exploits, yet they knew him from the radio and would answer his questions with politeness and respect. Managers, and I include the likes of Alex Ferguson and Walter Smith – the former not the biggest fan of the BBC – would always stop and take time to talk to him. In fact, I was guilty on many an occasion of using Jimmy's presence to get to a manager who would probably not have spoken to me, particularly if his team had just lost! He once said to me, after an interview that maybe he thought wasn't all that good, that I should always 'look them in the eye', which seemed pretty good advice. This was a man who had experienced both sides of the microphone, so I listened and did exactly what he told me.

Jimmy covered just about every big game and every big tournament with the BBC, mostly alongside the likes of Mike Ingham and Alan Green. He attended the top European fixtures, the Euro tournaments and the World Cups, although 2002 in Japan and South Korea was actually covered from his bedroom in Blackpool due to a knee injury! When the upcoming football fixtures were discussed at Television Centre on the Monday and the commentary team was chosen for the Saturday, then Jimmy's name was an automatic decision. There was no one quite like him and the only time he would not be the first choice as a summariser would be if the game was south of Birmingham, as he was reluctant to travel too far in later years.

I remember one extraordinary conversation I had on the phone with him one weekday midway through the season. As a football producer at the time, I was looking for a few new voices to do the analysis alongside the commentators but had not made any decisions as to which would be stood down (not that I had that amount of power!) and Jimmy rang me unexpectedly. He rang to ask if everything was okay and was he doing a good enough job? I was stunned. Of course he was. Why would he ask such a thing? He replied that he was grateful I'd said that and I must let him know if he wasn't up to standard anymore.

Now, here is one of the greatest footballers England has ever produced, a man who had captained England, a man who had managed a team in the European Cup Final and a man who had become one of the most well-known, loved and respected broadcasters in football ... and he was asking *me* if he was doing a good job? I may have been his producer but my standing alongside him was that of an irritating mosquito buzzing around a lion. It did again go to show how humble and self-effacing he really was. He hadn't contacted me for any ego massage or for a confirmation as to how good he was, it was because he was genuinely asking himself the questions. It was a moment that stayed with me for a long time.

Alongside Alan Green, the football correspondent of BBC Sport, Mike Ingham spent a long time working with Jimmy and travelling around the world with him. Mike recently wrote his memoirs after retiring from broadcasting and kindly gave permission to include this extract from *After Extra Time and Penalties*. This is what he had to say about his time with Jimmy:

(By kind permission of Mike Ingham – extract from *After Extra Time and Penalties*)

I first met him on Friday, 18 October 1963. It was the day before Blackpool's home game against Ipswich and we were having a family half-term illuminations holiday on the Golden Mile. Being the precocious 13-year-old that I was, I informed my folks that I was off to Bloomfield Road in the hope of seeing the players after training. One by one they came out and signed my book. Alan Ball, Ray Charnley, Tony Waiters, but still no sign of my main target and I wasn't going to leave until I had the autograph of the England captain. When Jim did eventually emerge in his car, I was standing at the wrong exit and had to do a personal best for the 100m sprinting in his direction. Jim saw me coming; he could hardly have missed me hurtling towards him and he waited understandingly for my breathless arrival. He opened his window, took my book and signed. When I told him this story 20 years later, he said that he had considered telling me to 'bugger off'. That would have been an impossibility. It was not part of his metabolism.

If there is one picture that sums up the spirit of Jimmy Armfield, it is the one of him on the Wembley pitch as a squad member at the end of the 1966 World Cup Final. There is not one ounce of visible disappointment at not being in the winning England team who are about to be presented with the trophy. There is only unbridled joy and pride to be part of something that may never ever be repeated, even though there would be no medal on that day to show for his involvement. The honour for the country overrode all other self-interest and he was like that as a summariser. I probably worked with Jimmy more than any other summariser and never once did he make it about himself and say anything for effect. It was always only about the game and having been there himself as a distinguished player. He knew it was a tough profession and, so, was never over critical but everything he did say carried the weight of sage authority. I would look forward to a commentary even more than usual if I knew that Jimmy was going to be sitting alongside me.

This would be a typical Sunday afternoon matchday with him in the north-west. Jim would enter the press room about 90 minutes before kick-off after having chatted to supporters outside the ground. Off would come his flat cap, a quick comb through what remained of his hair, cheery greetings all round and then, after firmly shaking my hand, he would say 'Well son, if they play as well this afternoon as I did this morning, then we're in for a good game', a reference to his shift on the church organ at morning prayers. More often than not, you would then be treated to a rendition of his latest joke, vintage end-of-the-pier stuff in the grand tradition of all those great Lancashire comedians. It was never blue and would nearly always start with 'This chap goes to the doctor'. After delivering the punchline, still chuckling, he would grab hold of you and insist 'It's a good 'un that, did you like it?' Of course, you loved it because he did. In the commentary, he would have a few pet phrases and the one that I associate most of all with him was when he used to say 'He's what I call …' Occasionally, like all of us attempting live radio, he might get his wires twisted and once observed about Aston Villa's Tony Morley 'He's what I call a down-and-out winger'.

When we were together in Budapest for a European game between Honvéd and Manchester United, he was recognised in our hotel by a rather portly old boy who came over and gave him a bear hug. They had played against each other at Wembley in 1963 when Jimmy had captained England against the Rest of the World. It had turned out to be one of the greatest footballers of all time and, although Ferenc Puskás didn't speak English, the two men conversed in the language of football, ending with Jimmy playfully prodding the great Hungarian in the tummy. The so-called 'Galloping Major' had developed a galloping middle-aged spread.

When he was commissioned by the FA to headhunt for two England managers, I naively assumed that, as his friend, I would be given special favours and the odd steer about who was likely to be appointed. I called him many times and we would chat at length. At the end of the call, I would look at my notepad and realise that nothing had been written down. This man of integrity had demonstrated why the FA had put their trust in him. When it was his 70th birthday in 2005, I was invited by the Blackpool Supporters' Club to make a speech at a special dinner in his honour at Bloomfield Road. Sir Tom Finney was also there, as were Jim's

England team-mates from Blackburn, Ronnie Clayton and Bryan Douglas. Everyone there that night got a stick of tangerine Blackpool rock with Jimmy's name on it to commemorate the occasion. That was Jimmy Armfield, 'The Blackpool Rock'. He would no doubt have been asked to approve the menu that night and insist that there should be no sauces or fancy stuff to spoil the taste. 'Don't put anything on it,' he would tell a puzzled maître d' at France 98. Jimmy belonged to the John Wayne school of fine dining when ordering his steak. 'Just wipe its bottom and put it on the plate'.

When still a teenager, Jimmy attended the Matthews Cup Final in 1953 between Blackpool and Bolton. Nearly 60 years later, he was guest of honour at the FA Cup Final between Chelsea and Liverpool, handing over the trophy to Frank Lampard and John Terry. I am able to say with great pride that when I did my final broadcast for the BBC in the summer of 2016, half a century on from the Boys of 66, I was able to work for one last time with Jimmy Armfield.

There will be some who will ask why Jimmy carried on? Why did he continue? He had been involved in football from the time he was a teenager, playing with youth teams before his big break with Blackpool. Seven decades later, he was still involved. He didn't need the money, even though he played at a time when the top players were not paid the bank vaults of cash that modern players take for granted and also demand, and even if he had needed the money, the BBC was never the corporation to make enough to retire on. All of his contemporaries had come and gone. Some had burst on to the radio scene, made their impact and then disappeared just as quickly. Others had seen it as a step to a position within the game once more, whilst a few had decided that the glamour of television was too much to ignore. Not Jimmy. He *loved* working on the radio. He loved getting up on a Saturday and making the journey to Anfield or Old Trafford or even Elland Road again, just so he could watch another football match and talk about it. Maybe it reminded him of his playing days and the Saturday routine, where he would get up at eight, have a light breakfast of toast and tea and then make his way to the ground? Maybe there was a deep yearning for the thrill of the packed stadiums again? Whatever his reasons, he was the most reliable professional that worked for the football team at BBC Radio. If you asked him to go to a certain game, he would go. Simple as that.

I personally loved it when I was working at a game when Jimmy was present. It wasn't just because he made my life easier, knowing that the post-match interview would be far more attainable with him at my side (and he used to love to come to the interviews and, without being asked, would take the microphone and do the interview himself) but it was also because I could spend time with him talking about Blackpool! I remember one famous moment (for me that is) when we were in the press room at Goodison Park ahead of the Merseyside derby. The day before (the game was being played on a Sunday for television coverage), Blackpool had lost 2-1 at home to Hartlepool United. I had attended and, in my mind, my beloved Tangerines should not even be playing a league game against the likes of Hartlepool, never mind losing to them! He listened to my rants and ravings about the incompetence of the team and the accident-prone club we supported and then, when I'd stopped talking, he just looked at me, shook his head gently and said 'It'll be okay, lad. I've seen it all before and more as not, I'll see it again. There's nothing to worry about.' He then went on to produce his usual expert commentary and analysis of Liverpool's comfortable victory over Everton. That was Jimmy.

Chapter 21:

The eloquence of simplicity

IN HIS book *Saturday 3pm – Fifty Eternal Delights of Modern Football* – Daniel Gray devotes a whole chapter to Jimmy Armfield and his voice. He says that: 'His regular tone is soft but serious, a measured grandad explaining why stealing is wrong. Volume rises to express annoyance at a cynical foul (Armfield did have one booking late in his career!) or glee at a wave of attacking play from a team chasing a goal … His is a blurring brogue which resonates with depth and honesty, where so much else now is sensation and surface.'

What is it about Jimmy's ability to speak in an eloquent and understandable style, especially as most footballers, no matter which era they came from, struggle to put one sentence after another? Even if they can, it's usually the old cliched 'one game at a time' or 'as long as we got the three points' type banality. Despite the modern trend of putting virtually every top player through intensive media training (which certainly makes a lot of money for former television and radio presenters), instilling just a modicum of personality is far more difficult. This is where Jimmy always had a head start.

He was always at ease in front of a microphone. It probably had a lot to do with his early training. Even as a player, he was often called into the BBC studios post-match to give his opinions. He was asked far more than any other Blackpool player because he was just about the only one who knew what to say! If you ever had the opportunity of attending an after-dinner speech by him, you would have seen how comfortable and engaging he really was. The Jimmy who tapped me on the shoulder in the car in Belgium as I was driving, just to remind me that the speed limit signs appeared to be something I'd been oblivious to, was the Jimmy who stood before an audience who were demanding to be entertained. He was just Jimmy.

Chris Hull – a Blackpool supporter for life and sports broadcaster amongst other things – held a dinner for the late Stan Mortensen in 2004 at Layton Institute in Blackpool. Jimmy was the main guest speaker and the person they'd all waited to hear from. There were cigars and brandy and expectation as he took to the stand and just listening back to the ten minutes or so of his speech showed how he was able to engage with virtually everyone present. He started it by poking fun at how he was now being perceived by the Blackpool public. He said that when he retired, he was described as the former Blackpool and England full-back. Ten years later in the 1980s, he was the 'Seasiders' World Cup star' and now he was just 'legend'! It made everyone laugh but it came easily to him, even when he described himself as being 'the late Jimmy Armfield' in 20 years' time.

Later, he told two stories about 'Morty'. They were delivered in his soft and gentle Lancashire brogue, even if, by this time, his vocal chords were beginning to show the signs of the disease that was starting to take hold. However, if one were to read a transcript of these stories, you would be able to 'hear' Jimmy speak. The first was about diving in the modern game and he joked that if 'Morty' fell over in Rigby Road, he'd somehow get into the opposition box and claim a penalty! The second was a typical Jimmy story – the kind I and my colleagues heard so many times in press rooms around the country. He told the tale of when Mortensen was following him on the M6 and started to flash his lights at Jimmy to pull over. This bemused and worried Jimmy, thinking there was some kind of crisis, and he pulled over at the next service station, concerned that 'Morty' had some bad news or needed advice. It was neither. Stan had pulled him over to tell him a joke! The joke? It's one that I heard numerous times and one that former Blackpool star Tony Green recounted to me during a phone conversation about Jimmy.

> Fella goes into the library. He says to the librarian 'Have you got any books on suicide?' The librarian says, 'Yes. Just go along the corner, turn right and second shelf.' He comes back and says, 'There's no books there' and the librarian looks at him and says, 'It's funny, they never bring them back …'

This was Jimmy. He spoke to the listener the way he spoke to you. Yes, he brought copious amounts of notes, as he always liked to be prepared, but his knowledge of the game was such that he could lose those notes and he would still be able to remember what he wanted to say. He was like your grandfather sat next to you, telling you what had just happened, but seeing something that you hadn't. You've just watched a player shimmy to the left and then unleash a shot that burst the net from 30 yards. Jimmy would then point out that, by shimmying to the left, another defender moved out of position, so the gap was there for the player to take the shot. He knew it because he'd played it and, whilst other ex-footballers would struggle to describe what they had just seen, he did it with calmness and authority. It didn't matter that most of his listeners were too young to remember him playing, or even managing; he spoke to everyone at their level. He needed no training and there was never once a single time that I, or any of the other producers, would need to correct him. He just knew.

This ability to speak and engage everyone wasn't just confined to football. His faith, of which we will come back to later in the book, was something he was passionate about. Never one to force his opinions on anyone, he was ready to discuss it when it was required. The Reverend Damien Feeney – who was part of the parish where Jimmy attended church – had this to say:

> As a child, I was taught that Jimmy Armfield was the nearest thing to a football deity that there was. Jimmy delivered, for his club, his community, his country, his church and the game itself.
>
> In 1999, I was leading a parish mission in Blackpool, and there was a men's evening in the local pub. There were two local Christian speakers: Jimmy and the comedian Syd Little. I was able to sit next to Jimmy

for the meal and he said to me, 'I've never spoken at anything like this: what do you want?' I asked him to talk about his faith and just to be himself. What followed was a revelation. After I introduced him, he stood up and the room was completely hushed to hear the great man. He spoke in simple, unaffected terms, leaving no one in any doubt that the life of the Christian was the only way he could travel. He was incredible. I will never forget it.

Jimmy continued to commentate and report for the BBC, even after he was diagnosed with cancer. The trio of the dignified and calm Mike Ingham, the firebrand and opiniated Alan Green and serene and knowledgeable Jimmy, was a combination which was hard to beat, but others also worked alongside Jimmy. To bring this chapter of his broadcasting career to an end, I'll let John Murray – BBC football commentator – to add his words of tribute:

When I first sat down to commentate next to Jimmy in the late 1990s, I felt like I had been listening to him on the radio for decades. And that's because I had. My memory of Jimmy's career in football was really limited to him as the face on a Panini sticker as the manager of Leeds United. I wasn't old enough to have actually seen Jimmy or any of his teams play but, nevertheless, by the time we worked together, I knew very well of the great many things he had achieved.

But my first-hand memories of him are as a broadcaster and, after all, I think I'm right in saying he had a longer career as a broadcaster than he did as a player and manager.

Jimmy loved the written and the spoken word and was a natural communicator with a gentle sense of humour. I think – in common with almost everyone who picks up a microphone – there was an ego there as well and I believe he enjoyed the profile working with the BBC gave him.

But he was also exclusively identified with the BBC. If you were listening to Jimmy, you knew it was BBC Radio. That's something that, in the modern crowded football media world, is now almost unheard of among the former players and managers-turned-broadcasters – to be exclusive.

And Jimmy was a broadcaster. His primary role was as the summariser, as we call it at the BBC, but over the years he reported on matches, conducted interviews and also presented programmes.

But as a summariser, he developed his own style. Because of what he'd achieved, he had a natural authority. And he also had a very pleasant broadcasting voice; soft, with his Lancashire accent. And it was also a voice that as he grew older remained constant – it didn't sound as old as he was. Even after his tangle with throat cancer, remarkably his voice seemed almost unaffected.

He was never an 'it was better in my day' man, even if he did think that. His enthusiasm for the game never seemed to wane. Whatever the match was, Jimmy would be up for it and would arrive with his little notebook in which he had written down the teams he expected to play. Anyone who worked alongside Jimmy for any length of time could not fail to pick up some of his pearls of wisdom. He would always talk about the star players as being the ones who, if you found out they weren't playing, left you feeling short-changed that you would not be seeing them play that day. A simple truism that is still as relevant today as it was when Jimmy was a player.

But when I say he had his own style of summarising, it would include phrases and hallmarks that were unique to him. Things like 'What happened there was …', which would be preceded by a pause. That was when Jimmy was telling the listener he was about to give them the definitive version and judgment on whatever had just happened.

'That's what I call …' A little like the above. So, if it was, say, 'a bad tackle', the listener would know that because, if Jimmy called it that way, it really must be. 'Ahmeenahsay' (translation: I mean to say). Jimmy often began sentences this way, which again served to underline the importance of what was about to follow. Sometimes he would alternatively pause and give a little cough before delivering his verdict, for the same effect.

'Ah thought ah was right.' One of my favourites, used when the subsequent replay on the TV in the commentary position confirmed whatever it was Jimmy had already said. And, of course, the classic 'I was right behind that.' Whenever there was an attempt on goal

Jimmy had seen from that angle, this phrase would almost always be used.

Even now, very rarely does a month of the football season go by when I will not reference Jimmy for one reason or another during a football commentary. He had that much of an influence on us. When you sat next to Jimmy, you knew you were in good hands because of what he had seen and done in the game. Because of that, he remained relevant into his later years. And whatever unexpected, controversial or dramatic happening might occur, there was a confidence that Jimmy would always take it in his stride and find the right words. He was the ultimate commentator's summariser.

Chapter 22:

The FA and England

ONE OF the aspects of Jimmy's life that sometimes tends to be overlooked was his role at the FA and, in particular, his part in the appointment of two England managers. It was at a time when England had failed again. Spectacularly, but then that could have been said at other times, too. They'd failed to qualify for the 1994 World Cup and manager Graham Taylor had done the only thing that was left for him and had resigned. The vitriol that had been heaped on to his head, especially by the media, had almost ruined him.

It showed that the old saying that the England manager's job was more difficult than that of prime minister was probably not too much of an exaggeration. Taylor had tried and failed. Now England needed another manager. They needed someone who could stare the Three Lions in the eye and dare them to prove themselves again following the whimper of the previous few years. England needed saving and they turned to Jimmy Armfield.

It wasn't quite as straightforward or as romantic as that, but the FA, in the shape of the rather dour Graham Kelly, appealed to Jimmy's sense of English patriotism and his obvious knowledge of football.

Jimmy told the story of a November day in 1993 when, while working diligently in his £18,000-a-year job as a journalist at the *Daily Express*, he was told by one of the secretaries at the Manchester office that there was a Mr Kelly on the phone asking to speak to him. That turned out to be Blackpool fanatic and FA chief executive Graham Kelly. He wanted to know if Jimmy was going to be at Old Trafford the following evening for the game between Manchester United and Ipswich Town, to which Jimmy replied that he would be and that he would be supplying the BBC Radio analysis. That was perfect for Kelly and he quickly persuaded Jimmy to meet him at lunchtime before the game, as he had something to ask him.

Now, let's just take a pause and consider what was about to happen here. England, the inventor of the game of soccer but unable to stamp its authority on those who had learned from them and bettered them, were now missing from the biggest tournament in the world for the third time in the last six. The Three Lions had stopped roaring and the supporters had turned off their televisions and pretended that the USA had no right to be hosting a football World Cup anyway, so they wouldn't watch. England needed a new manager, so it was probably taken for granted that the most scientific and intense approach was about to be made by footballing experts up and down the country. Data would be compiled, facts would be checked and rechecked, films of games would be watched and virtually every manager in the country's top league would be interviewed. They would be sounded out, tested and put through the rigorous process of selection to find the man who would take England to the heights they always believed were a given, not an exception. It actually wasn't like that at all. Instead, they asked Jimmy to find them one.

There doesn't seem to be a record of any of the conversations that must have taken place between the committee members of the FA, where it was decided that a former England captain and now a radio pundit would be responsible for one of the biggest decisions in international football. As mentioned earlier, it has been said that being the manager of England is at times more stressful than being the prime minister of the UK and it was down to Jimmy to find that man. It wasn't that Jimmy wasn't up to the task but when Graham Kelly ended their lunch meeting by saying, 'Right, off you go. Go and find us a new manager,' it must have seemed a little surreal. Jimmy then had to get back to the mundane job of watching Manchester United and Ipswich Town play out a goalless draw. It proved, though, that life had its surprises.

So, Jimmy now worked for the FA. He didn't need to relocate to London, as there were offices in Manchester, but he did have one specific brief and that was to find the country a new football manager. How he kept that particular piece of information from his newspaper journalist colleagues is a mystery, and quite impressive, but he certainly took the task extremely seriously. The problem was, who on earth was qualified to take on such a role? After the painful public humiliation of Graham Taylor at the end of 1993, he needed to find someone who was able to deal with top-class players, cope with the pressure of the job and the constant scrutiny from the press and who had the ability to turn an underperforming nation into the world-beaters (or at least Euro 96-beaters) that the supporters were demanding. There weren't too many candidates.

After speaking to FA chairman Bert Millichip and the members of the international committee – Noel White of Liverpool, Ian Stott of Oldham Athletic and Peter Swales of Manchester City – it was clear that they all had different views on who they thought would be a suitable candidate. The list was short. Firstly, there was absolutely no chance of there being a non-English manager. The days of Sven were some way off. That eliminated half of the top managers in the country. Also, Ron Atkinson, for reasons never made too clear, was a definite non-starter, so the final ten are a glimpse of a 1990s that seems to exist only in the early days of the Sky-invented Premiership. Baggy shirts, with huge advertising slogans, and Richard Keys wearing a yellow jacket to present the Monday night game. We had Gerry Francis, Glenn Hoddle, Howard Kendall, Peter Reid, Howard Wilkinson, Joe Royle, Trevor Francis, Billy Bonds, Ray Wilkins and Bryan Robson, only one of whom would go on to receive the glittering prize, although he had to wait a little while. There was no Terry Venables on the list at the time, as his business dealings following his departure from Tottenham Hotspur were seen to be an obstacle, especially to the wise old men of the FA committee. It was hardly encouraging.

It didn't take long for the inquisitive press to find out what Jimmy was up to. They followed him and harried him. They tailed his car and they listened to every word he spoke when on the radio. They needed to know – before anyone else, of course

– who he had chosen as the new England manager and they had little interest in patience. Thankfully, Jimmy didn't reveal anything but that was also because he actually didn't know!

He spoke to them all. He spoke to Gerry Francis in his hotel bedroom but lost interest after the constant references to the pressure that the Queens Park Rangers manager feared. He spoke to both Bryan Robson and Ray Wilkins, but neither were ready for such a big step. Both were still playing and their major managerial opportunities were a few years away. He spoke to Trevor Francis, but wasn't convinced by him, and he spoke to Howard Kendall, who just wasn't interested. Joe Royle was dismissed, as was Howard Wilkinson, which was surprising bearing in mind his association with the national team. The last one was Glenn Hoddle, but Jimmy, as wise as ever, decided he wasn't quite ready just yet. He'd been a success at Swindon Town but had only recently joined Chelsea, a far bigger club, and needed to prove himself there before any move to the international scene. Jimmy was lost, unless he could persuade the committee to choose Terry Venables, which seemed a pretty unlikely happening at that stage. To Jimmy, though, he was the only real candidate, so he went on a campaign to garner support, enlisting the help of some of the top names in the game.

He spent time talking to the likes of Alex Ferguson, Bobby Robson, Gordon Taylor of the PFA and others, such as Johnny Giles and Graham Taylor – the latter being very generous with his advice, bearing in mind he'd just been booted from the position Jimmy was trying to fill! It was clear that Venables was becoming the only candidate that Jimmy was pursuing and soon the press became aware, too. Venables was 'the people's choice', as Brian

Clough was back in the 70s and Kevin Keegan was later to become. Jimmy told the story of how he was working at a Grimsby Town match when suddenly he was assailed by fans who insisted that he appoint Venables. Unfortunately, that groundswell opinion didn't reach as far as some members of the FA committee. Peter Swales, in particular, seemed to be totally against the idea. Later, once Venables had been appointed, the MP, Kate Hoey, made a statement in the House of Commons detailing why Venables was not a good choice for the next England manager. That surely went to show how important this role was!

The problem with Venables was that he had 'baggage', despite his obvious qualities as a football coach. There was a fallout over his time as Tottenham Hotspur chief executive, following his move upstairs from the manager's office. He'd actually tried to buy the club but had accepted a role under the new owner, Alan Sugar. This, of course, had ended in acrimony and, with his numerous business dealings, it was felt by many that he wasn't what was required. In fact, when Bobby Robson had departed from the job some years earlier, Venables hadn't even reached the last three candidates due to his business profile. Jimmy didn't see it that way and he was only interested in Terry Venables the football man.

> I arranged to meet Terry outside Euston Station in his Mercedes. He hadn't shaved and his car was full of the smell of garlic. I got the impression he'd had a good night out the previous evening and I felt he'd probably not slept since! it was so strong, the smell that is, that I offered him a stick of chewing gum to douse down the

fumes every time he opened his mouth, but he wasn't interested. Anyway, that was Terry. So, we drove to the Royal Lancaster Hotel and spent a couple hours there. He was good company and I was impressed with his football knowledge, which was a given, really. I met him and his wife where they lived in Hammersmith and it was clear that Terry wanted the job and I felt he could definitely do it, too … I decided I would recommend him.

His football credentials couldn't really be questioned. As well as being a very successful player, who had represented England, his managerial career had also been a success. He'd taken Crystal Palace to promotion, managed Queens Park Rangers to promotion and an FA Cup Final, led Barcelona to a European Cup Final for the first time since 1961 and had made progress at Tottenham Hotspur before taking an 'upstairs' role. This was the Terry Venables that Jimmy was interested in.

It took a few committee meetings and lots of persuasion by Jimmy for Venables to finally become the new England manager – or coach as Venables insisted on being called – and it was very much a Jimmy Armfield appointment. Basically, if Terry failed, then it was pretty much Jimmy's fault but loyalty counted for a lot in Jimmy's life and he gave Venables that loyalty and expected exactly the same in return. On 28 January 1994, Venables faced the voracious press as the new England coach, with Don Howe and Bryan Robson as his assistants. It had taken three months of interviewing, listening, chasing and persuading but Jimmy Armfield had done what Graham Kelly had asked and he had found England a new manager.

Chapter 23:

Find another one

WITH HIS job done, Jimmy returned to more mundane duties at the FA, as well as continuing his radio work. He watched from afar as Venables prepared for the Euro 96 tournament, the first big footballing event held in England since the 1966 World Cup finals. Jimmy actually attended Venables's first game in charge, a 1-0 win over the current European champions Denmark at Wembley in March 1994. He said that he didn't normally suffer from nerves as either a player or manager but that the kittens were stirring in his stomach as Venables sat on the bench. Thankfully, Jimmy was able to throw his flat cap into the air when the only goal of the game was scored by David Platt. It was all going to be okay.

How many wondered how Jimmy felt when he sat at Wembley Stadium for the Euro 96 tournament and if it brought back memories of 30 years earlier? It was another tournament where he played a major role without really being at the heart of it. Of course, England played superbly in two games – against the Netherlands and Germany – and didn't actually lose a game, only to be eliminated in the semi-finals on penalties by the

Germans. It was bitterly disappointing for everyone, especially as there really seemed to be a synchronicity about the 30 years, Wembley and winning something. Sadly, football rarely does sentiment and England walked away with the usual 'what might have been' feeling.

Unfortunately, even before the tournament started, Jimmy was on the lookout for another manager/coach! Venables, never one to be predictable, had told Graham Kelly at the Euro 96 finals draw in Birmingham in December 1995 that he wouldn't be pursuing a new contract. He felt that he hadn't been given the backing he deserved and the questions over his business interests were becoming louder and longer. He affirmed his decision a few weeks later when Noel White had countered the general enthusiasm for him staying by saying he felt Venables needed to prove himself first and end some of his business interests. Terry said 'no' and he made the announcement that he would walk away at the end of the tournament. That's what he did and the committee of businessmen and football chairmen had to turn to Jimmy once more in their quest to find someone who wasn't involved in business and knew a lot about football. As Jimmy said, he was a 'headhunter' again.

There was only one person that Jimmy seriously considered and that was Glenn Hoddle. Having said that, if things had worked out differently, the whole direction of English football could have changed.

One of the people who Jimmy regularly spoke to was Alex Ferguson at Manchester United. They had become friends and often after a game where Jimmy was reporting or summarising, he would spend time with him in his office. I remember how well they got on and there was always a smile and a handshake when the two of them met, usually at Old Trafford after a game. Whereas I would be given a look of utter contempt because of my association with the BBC (Ferguson never did warm to us), Jimmy was welcomed with open arms and a cup of tea. It was during such meetings that Jimmy sought Ferguson's views on Hoddle and whether he felt that the current Chelsea manager would be a good fit for England. It's never been reported what was discussed, as Jimmy wouldn't be one to break a confidence, but he did confirm that he jokingly asked Alex if he fancied the England job!

Now, the thought of a Scotsman managing England or an Englishman managing Scotland is anathema to most and, of course, this was at a time when England hadn't had anyone outside of the country become their manager, but it seems that Alex may have shown an interest. That was followed by Jimmy mentioning this to Graham Kelly, who then made an official approach to Manchester United – something Jimmy says he wasn't aware of. No progress was made, though, as United were the dominant force in the domestic game at the time, winning title after title and about to embark on a second European Cup/ Champions League success, so chairman Martin Edwards refused permission for the FA to interview Ferguson. He also made sure the Scot was given a hefty increase in his contract, which worked out perfectly for him. Ferguson did concede, though, many years later, that he would have liked to have spoken about the job a little bit more. Such moments ...

So, Glenn Hoddle was given the job. It wasn't as straightforward as that, though. There were many meetings in

London, some sat in Hyde Park with Hoddle or at his house at Epsom with his wife and children, but eventually Jimmy recommended him as the new England manager. Hindsight is always a great thing to have but if you read some of the comments that Jimmy made at the time, it is clear that there was a small matter of doubt that was eating away at him all the time. He described Hoddle as 'arrogant at times' and 'opinionated' but he felt he was thick-skinned enough to deal with whatever pressures came with the most important job in English football. Jimmy saw Hoddle as a footballing man who'd had an amazing playing career, was knowledgeable about the sport and well-travelled enough to know how to deal with foreign games and tournaments. He was a family man and that seemed to be very important to Jimmy, as that was the epitome of himself. Hoddle was the man, even if Jimmy didn't appear to be totally convinced. Hoddle recalled in a BBC Radio 5 Live interview:

> I remember to this day taking the call and meeting up with Jimmy. It was amazing. I was shocked at the time, I've got to say. He was very brave at even thinking of me at that time. I'd only had four years of experience as a manager and I was only 39 years of age. I remember saying, 'Are you sure about this, Jimmy?' He had a lot of faith in me and he reassured me that I would be the man for him. I owe a lot to Jimmy, I really do … We lost at home to Italy … back in the office on the Monday, the first person who came in, and he'd come from up north, he came straight into the office and he was there for us … We had a cup of tea and he said,

'Look, do you think you can still qualify [for the 1998 World Cup]' and I said 'Yes, I think I do'. A big smile came over his face and he said, 'If you believe it, then we can do it.' That was the man at his very, very best ... it was the support of people like Jimmy that gave me the inner belief that we can do it.

It was clearly an odd and uncomfortable situation having a new England manager appointed whilst the old one was still working, but Hoddle was announced just before the Euro 96 tournament. He did meet up with the players briefly at an England training camp but the awkwardness was probably all too obvious, as Venables was still preparing for the tournament. Anyway, Jimmy had supplied England with their second manager/coach in two years, so his job was done.

Hoddle's reign was both successful and controversial. He managed to get England to the 1998 World Cup at the expense of Italy in the group stage, which was no mean feat. Leaving France 98 at the quarter-final stage on penalties against Argentina in Saint-Étienne was less than was expected but that game was, in a way, a microcosm of England and their inability to find success. His departure from the role was, of course, clouded in accusations, ridicule and anger. It's openly documented as to why Hoddle was forced to resign in 1999 and there is little point in repeating it here in a book about Jimmy Armfield but it was notable that the next England manager was chosen without Jimmy's input.

Kevin Keegan took on the role – another of the 'people's favourite' variety – but Jimmy wasn't involved in the decision to offer him the job, initially on a caretaker basis and then full-time. Was this the FA showing they no longer trusted his judgment? Maybe that is harsh because, after all, Jimmy could only recommend a person; he wasn't responsible for either employing him or managing his abilities whilst in the job. It is fair to say, though, that Jimmy was not consulted at all about Keegan and, as he said in his autobiography: 'If I'd been consulted, I might have counselled against rushing it.'

Jimmy's role in the FA was wide and ranging. He was a consultant to the chief executive, was involved himself in coaching and, under Howard Wilkinson, played a large part in the St Georges Park National Football Centre project that opened near Burton-upon-Trent in 2002. He had visited the French equivalent – which had been hugely successful for many years – at Clairefontaine and met the former French and Liverpool coach Gérard Houllier, who was in charge at the time. French football was on a high after winning the 1998 World Cup and the opportunity of seeing how they did it was one that couldn't really be turned down.

His main commitment at the FA, though, was the development of a coaching scheme for players who wanted to go into management. This he did from his Manchester offices and it is clearly something that was close to his heart. One fact that is hidden amongst the gems of Jimmy's life is that, when he was still a player, he had actually attended coaching sessions as a prelude to becoming a manager once he had retired. This was not quite the expected route for players in the 1970s, as most of them just hung up their boots and put on a training suit and immediately became a manager. It worked with some – such as Brian Clough – but it probably failed to work with most others. Jimmy had the vision to see that he had to take care of himself and his family. So, once the playing days had left him behind, he had journalism and the possibility of coaching to fall back on. The kind of problem that today's highly paid, cradled and pampered superstars have barely given a second's thought to. Different times.

There is one happy note to end this chapter on, though. When Sven Göran Eriksson was appointed as England's first non-English manager (following the abrupt and early resignation of Kevin Keegan), he met up with Jimmy. After some polite conversation, Sven said unexpectedly that he could tell that Jimmy didn't remember him. Obviously, Jimmy didn't but it transpired that when Sven was learning how to become a football coach, he'd written to the top clubs in Europe asking if he could spend a few days watching how they trained and how the managers dealt with the players. Jimmy was manager at Leeds United at the time and he'd said 'yes'. Sven spent two days there and so, in a way, Jimmy also had a hand in the appointment of the Swede.

It's worth wondering, too, what kind of manager Jimmy would have made if he'd been given the chance with England. When he left Leeds United, his stock was very high and he himself said he'd finally become the manager that he wanted to be, but he walked away from that career. It may never have happened but, at a time when England were failing spectacularly, Jimmy Armfield could have been that calm and serene force that guided them to better times. He'd captained England and I'm sure he could easily have managed England. In an alternate universe, he did both … and successfully.

Chapter 24

The family man

ONE OF the consistent threads throughout this biography is the one that refers to Jimmy as a family man. It's not forced and it's not an attempt to make him out to be a modern-day saint or something remarkably special. It's simply because it is exactly what Jimmy was. He was a family man and his family always came first. His devotion to his wife, Anne, was well known and his two sons, Duncan and John, adored him. I spoke to Duncan about his father and it was clear from the emotion in his voice that Jimmy was a special dad. He told me of a letter Jimmy had written to his sons (of which the contents are private and not to be released), in which he promised that they would never have to worry financially and that he would always take care of them. The fact that he refused to relocate from Blackpool when he was made manager of Leeds United, preferring to make the lengthy commute over the rather challenging Pennines, says a lot for his devotion. I know, as his football producer for a few years, that when I was scheduling which games he was attending, it was always north of Birmingham. It was simply so he could return home at the end of the day.

Home? It was Blackpool and nowhere else. As someone who was brought up in the town, I at times find it hard to look at the place with any real feeling of attachment and belonging. The promenade, despite extensive restoration, is still the preserve of amusement arcades, candy floss, toffee apples and gypsy Rosa Lee parlours. The 'kiss me quick' hats have been replaced by something more vulgar and the 'zero tolerance' promise of so many years ago became just a trendy phrase that politicians could use to appease the locals. A night out on a Saturday is an experience, with a public house on virtually every corner and barely a local to be seen as the hen parties and stag dos define Blackpool's entertainment credentials. Take a step back away from the seafront and you can see the poverty and lack of investment, with boarded-up shops and run-down bed and breakfast establishments. Unemployment is rife, personal wealth is non-existent and the alcohol and drug problems are there to stay. There is a beauty, though.

A walk along a deserted seven-mile golden-sanded beach, with the sun rising, the breeze bringing a tear to the eye and the tower looking down like a caring grandmother, is a pleasurable experience. Looking at the three piers as they stretch out to the sea, with their bingo halls and quaint advertising painted white on black roofs, the seagulls flying above, gives a glimpse of a British tradition that few want to lose. Also, a walk through the town can reveal so much more than the poverty and decay. It's true that the council is embarking on a huge redevelopment, with large swathes of the town centre changing beyond recognition. Even the trams are making their way back to the train station again, for the first time in decades. The Pleasure Beach still delights and, even in the cynical 21st century, the Illuminations are more than capable of putting a smile on a child's face.

The Blackpool of the packed beach, with deckchairs covering every inch of the yellow sand, is now a thing of the past but there is still beauty and magnificence. You just have to look a little more intently and make sure you 'push the door open' when searching for heart of the town.

Blackpool people are called 'Sandgrown'uns' and that's the part of the town that Jimmy and his family belong to. In the 1940s, the town was regarded as a 'paradise' by Jock Dodds when he joined the club from Sheffield United and even today there is something quite special about the place, if you allow yourself to let it seep into your consciousness. Jimmy lived there nearly all of his life, never really having the desire to move away, although if the big money move to Manchester United or Arsenal had taken place, then it would have been a huge temptation. For Jimmy, Blackpool was his home and it was his community.

A lot has been said and written about Jimmy's commitment to his community and, of course, the fact that every Sunday he could be found playing the church organ, something that seemed to be at odds with the lifestyle of a footballer, even all those years ago. There is so much more to discover, though, and it is here, more than anywhere else, that we see the real Jimmy Armfield. More than a footballer, more than a manager, more than a writer or a broadcaster, it's here. Jimmy as the family man. Jimmy as the man who played the church organ every Sunday and then took his wife and children to their holiday caravan in the Lake District. It's the beautiful ordinariness of his life. It's almost perfect and you dare to wonder that even if Jimmy hadn't reached the heights of his footballing career and had a job that was slightly more mundane, he would still have been at peace with his Sunday routine.

His organ playing came about due to the influence of the man who should always be credited with making Jimmy what he became. It was his father who 'forced', and forced is not too strong a word, Jimmy to take up piano lessons when he was just nine years of age and more interested in kicking a laced-up football against the gable ends of the house next door. In that early war period, when wearing shorts and hobnail boots and eating stew every Friday was the routine, Jimmy was being trained to prepare for a life that was to be anything but ordinary.

The piano lessons were from a Mr Jones across the road. Jimmy said he never knew his first name and never asked, either! It wasn't just piano lessons, though. Mr Jones (and no description is forthcoming but you can imagine a wax moustache, a three-piece suit and a pipe) made Jimmy learn about music before his hands were allowed anywhere near the piano keys. He had to learn how to write it, how to read it and the history of some of the great classical composers. It's due to this that he always loved classical music. He also had a fondness for musicals. Music played a big part in his life.

As a boy, the local Sunday school and youth club were a big part of his social life, both of them belonging to St Peter's Church in South Shore, Blackpool (a church which, in 2017, was sadly described as the most deprived parish in England), and it was here that he made his public debut as a piano player. At the age of 13, he was asked by the Sunday school manager,

Bert Ellis, if he would play a couple of hymns the following week, as their regular player had given up. It's fair to say that, alongside his debut for Blackpool and then that exhilarating, but nerve-racking first game for England against Brazil, playing the piano in front of all his friends on a Sunday morning was probably right up there in his life highlights list. According to his autobiography, he played hymn number 334, 'Loving Shepherd of Thy Sheep', and presumably played it well enough to keep the job until he was 16! If he was concerned about his image with his friends and peers, he needn't have been. In a far more innocent age, the sight of your pal playing a church piano on a Sunday morning was an arresting and pleasant one. I'm not sure that level of respect would be afforded today, sadly.

The church organ seemed to be mastered just as quickly and soon this young man, as well as being a promising footballer about to embark on a Blackpool and England career, was also the official organist for the local church in South Shore. Now, tell me, have you ever heard such a thing? He wasn't a regular (as church organist, that is) until the mid-70s, when there was a shortage of people possessing the talent Jimmy had, but it's amazing and a true testament to him that he continued playing for the next 40 years or so.

His faith was important to him. Instilled into him by his mother and father, he never missed a Sunday at church if he could help it. He spoke regularly at church meetings about it and even when he was interviewing Glenn Hoddle about the England job, he asked why the younger man didn't go to church when he had professed to believing in God. Faith was important and he managed to pass it down to his sons, too.

One of the pleasures he shared with his family was that of fell walking in the Lake District. Like a modern-day Wainwright, he would take Anne and his sons to the caravan as often as he could and they would just go walking. Jimmy said that you should never try to explore the Lake District by car, as it was a wasted opportunity, so walking boots were the order of the day. For those who are acquainted with the Lake District, there are few places in the United Kingdom that can compete with this area for its spectacular scenery and the peace, calm and tranquillity. I can imagine how Jimmy would go there regularly, as it was the exact opposite of the life he was leading in football. He even bought a boat but admitted that he let both Duncan and John commandeer it on many an occasion.

This sense of family is something that a lot of us can only admire and wish for, so it shows how hard he tried to make the family the most important thing in his life. No one lives a blameless life, as far as I can see, but he came as close as possible to achieving that. I can only imagine his reception at the Pearly Gates being a good and welcoming one.

His house in South Shore was modest, especially if you were to attempt to compare it to the multi-million pound penthouses that the latest stars have at their disposal, but it was welcoming and, as the years passed, Jimmy's face wasn't recognised as instantly as it used to be (although his name and certainly his voice were), so he was able to go for long walks without being harried by people taking photographs. Thankfully, the 'selfie' is a far more recent phenomenon and one which Jimmy wasn't faced with. Autograph hunters tended to be of an older generation but, of course, they had all now grown up and, therefore, showed him the respect he deserved.

The list of titles that Jimmy had in and around Blackpool and Lancashire is a testament to the respect he was held in and the work he put into the local community. For instance, he was a director of the National Health Service Trust board, something which initially amused wife Anne, who had been a nurse for 35 years and thought that this was the straw that would finally make the NHS back buckle. Thankfully, Jimmy's involvement was nowhere near as detrimental as that. He was also asked to be the director of the Blackpool Fylde and Wyre Hospital Trust, which accounts for nine hospitals, something which was very close to his heart, and of which some of the royalties from this book will be forwarded.

He became president of the local branch of Age Concern, the governor and chairman of Arnold School, the vice-president of Lancashire Outward Bound, chairman of the Lancashire Partnership Against Crime and there are so many more. In fact, if there is a Lancashire trust of any sort that didn't have Jimmy's name alongside it, then it's fair to say it should have done. Never has there been a more energetic and enthusiastic proponent of local affairs as the former captain of the England football team. Blackpool's gain, on the day that the young Jimmy Armfield arrived at North Station, shirt and jumper tucked into shorts, his eyes blinking away the steam from the engine and his lungs breathing in the purity of the sea air, was one that they could never not acknowledge. He was Mr Blackpool.

Chapter 25:

Honours, medals and bouquets

JIMMY WAS honoured. Of course he was. How could he not be? He was awarded the freedom of Blackpool in 2000, but that was a given. A man who devoted his life to the town couldn't not receive such an honour. It was the very least the town could do. At about the same time, he was finally recognised by Buckingham Palace and given an OBE. It was an immense honour and, even though he said years later that the honours bestowed him by the local community meant a bit more, there is no doubt the pride in which he (figuratively speaking) wore the OBE on his chest. It came out of the blue, according to Jimmy. An envelope and a letter and he was invited to the palace. One of those surreal moments that very few of us will ever experience. It was his moment and this is how he described the day he received it:

The investiture at Buckingham Palace was such a memorable occasion. The invitation specified that I should be accompanied by Anne and two guests, so Duncan and John came along. It was the perfect family occasion, because they are the most important things to me in the world. We stayed overnight at the Royal Garden Hotel in Kensington and they had kindly given us a suite for the price of a double room. I rarely stay in fancy hotels, so this was a bit of a treat, really. They then provided a chauffeur-driven Jaguar the next day.

I waited in an anteroom until called – Mr James Armfield, the OBE for services to association football. The band of the Blues and Royals were playing as I walked across the red carpet to meet the Prince of Wales, who shook me by the hand and said, 'I'm sorry it's taken so long to get you here' and then, 'Now, what are we going to do about this England football team?' Can you imagine that? He knew exactly what was happening with England. I didn't say much, because there were others behind me waiting, but I think I would have liked to have had a chat with him about football.

Ten years later, that OBE had been advanced to CBE, but the knighthood that all Blackpool supporters campaigned for throughout the years was never awarded. This wasn't something that particularly bothered him but it certainly bothered the fans of the club. The erection of a statue outside the ground that had a stand named after him (of which there will be more shortly) showed the affection they had and, even now, Jimmy is described as 'Sir Jimmy' when spoken of. Maybe one day that honour will be bestowed, many years after it should have been. After all, he finally received a World Cup winner's medal some

43 years after the event. In 2009, on 11 June, Jimmy and his non-playing colleagues finally received the medal that should have been handed out at Wembley in 1966. The insensitivity of the 1960s resolved and repaired in the 2000s.

So, what of the freedom of the town? An honour that in the modern age seems to remind us of days long past, when the title meant you could walk your sheep through the high street without being arrested or you could wear a ceremonial chain when attending public duties. It seems to our modern sensibilities an anachronism that no longer belongs ... but take a look at the past recipients and wonder in awe at the achievements of such people. Stan Mortensen, as much deserving as our own Jimmy, and probably regarded as Blackpool's greatest player. He is still the *only* man to have scored a hat-trick in an FA Cup Final and then had the glory of it taken off him unwittingly by his team-mate, who was bewitching the nation with his silky skills.

There was Field Marshal Montgomery, whose extraordinary achievements in the Second World War are now the subject of Hollywood-style film treatments, where sometimes the truth gets clouded over, but his leadership in the war is a school history lesson that should never be forgotten or overlooked. Then we have Sir Winston Churchill. As well as all of the plaudits and adulation and respect and just about everything else, the man who was arguably the country's greatest leader was also a freeman of Blackpool. Jimmy was in pretty good company.

Whereas the Buckingham Palace reception was inevitably quite formal, and it was only shared by Anne and his two sons, the Imperial Hotel reception was a little more fun. All of his friends, family and just about most who knew him were there and ready to congratulate. Both awards meant a great deal but you get the feeling that it was the one from his own backyard that probably meant just a little bit more. When the people you've lived amongst, or the people you've represented, the friends you've shared a laugh and a drink with, and even the ones you may have had a disagreement with, when all of these people come together to honour a special person in their midst, that must surely be the moment of immense pride.

The town of Blackpool, gaudy and vulgar at times, but boasting a true sense of community also, had as one of its citizens someone whose influence spread far and wide, almost around the globe. People said that in the 1950s if you mentioned Blackpool to anyone in any country, they would almost certainly reply 'Stanley Matthews'. Now, in later years, many would identify the town with Jimmy. The seaside resort could never have found a better public relations officer anywhere, even if it had tried. There were more mentions of Blackpool on BBC Radio in a week when he was broadcasting than if the tourism office had actually paid for them. I can't imagine the town ever having such a willing exponent of the values and the spirit of Blackpool ever again. Jimmy was unique. Blackpool loved him and he loved Blackpool. A perfect fit, really.

Chapter 26:

The final years

JIMMY CARRIED on working and continued to be as active as ever but, by 2007, his health had deteriorated. He announced in May of that year that he was now suffering from non-Hodgkin lymphoma, a cancer that had started to spread and had caused him serious health problems. He made a decision to retire from public life for a while as he fought it. It came at a time when his beloved Blackpool had started a renaissance and had made the play-off final for a return to the Championship for the first time in 29 years. Jimmy was sadly absent from the crowd at Wembley, as his tangerine favourites overwhelmed a spirited Yeovil Town and a curious-looking Latvian called Valeri Belekon (who had bought a stake in the club) then stood on the pitch afterwards wearing a tangerine tie and announced that Blackpool would be in the Premier League within five years. Most fans smiled indulgently but it almost certainly cheered up Jimmy.

Whilst he was recovering, he was awarded a place in the football 'Hall of Fame' at the National Football Museum, which in those days was based at Deepdale, home of Preston North End, who were, of course, Blackpool's main rivals. He was presented with the honour by his former England team-mate Jimmy Greaves, an award that was voted for by Bobby Charlton, Tom Finney and Mark Lawrenson amongst others.

Jimmy fought the cancer and won. Would you have expected anything else? He resumed his radio duties and carried on living his life as well as he could. Three years later, he was immensely honoured to have the newly built South Stand at Bloomfield Road named after him. The ground, a shambling wreck towards the end of its life, only a safety-certificate away from closure, was going through one of the longest rebuilds in the history of the game. The controlling Oyston family were holding on to the purse strings in a far more aggressive fashion than seen before. Already, there had been the Mortensen Stand and the Matthews Stand, so to have the Armfield Stand was an obvious direction to take. It was completed in May 2010 and Jimmy was there to cut the ceremonial ribbon.

It was a busy time for Jimmy and his original football love because, later that month, they beat Cardiff City 3-2 to gain promotion to the Premier League, again via a play-off final, proving that Mr Belekon seemed to know a thing or two about English football. This time, Jimmy was there, resplendent and smiling on a day when the sun shone brighter than at any other time of the year and the white-shirted Blackpool players celebrated the type of fairytale that only football seems capable of supplying in the sporting world. There even appeared to be a tear in his eye. Jimmy had played in the last top-tier fixture that Blackpool had competed in and now he was watching a whole new generation of players taking the club to a place that few thought they would ever see again. Now it was the time of Adam, Campbell, Ormerod and Taylor-Fletcher to carry on where Green, Suddick, Hutchison and Armfield had left off.

It didn't stop there. He was sufficiently healthy and fit enough to work alongside John Murray in the next season's opening fixture – away to Wigan Athletic. In a game that defied all of the pundits and delighted the neutrals, as well as the huge Blackpool support, the Tangerines won 4-0 and, for two hours, found themselves at the top of English football's league system. Jimmy, trying to be as unbiased as he could, allowed a little emotion when he threw his cap in the air as another Blackpool goal was scored. One of the beautiful moments of his life was him being able to see the team play in the Premier League alongside Manchester United, City, Arsenal and Liverpool. It was a great moment.

Those moments continued when, on 1 May 2011, a 9ft bronze statue was erected outside the ground and next to the stand that bore his name. It was a fitting tribute to the man who was Mr Blackpool. It dominates the south-west corner of the ground and is a magnet for fans, both home and visitors.

> I feel quite humble about it and I must be honest – I will be very proud to see it, as I am with the stand, as Blackpool is my team and my town. It is nice to think that anything I have done has been appreciated. All people like to think that.

Unlike the shameful treatment of the Stan Mortensen statue at the north stand by those who knew little of or cared little about football (and I am referring to the previous owners of the club, of which no mention in this book is deserved), Jimmy's statue has stood tall on the Bloomfield Road entrance. With the new supporters' club named after him, just a few yards away, it is clear the level of affection he has from all Blackpool supporters.

If you enter Bloomfield Road, there is the 'Hall of Fame', a decade-by-decade record of the fans' favourite players and, of course, Jimmy is there, his photograph displayed proudly in the 1960s section, and if that isn't enough, as just referred to, the local working men's club situated just a few yards from the ground was redeveloped and renamed … and you guessed it. It is now called 'The Armfield Club', with a huge mural of Jimmy on the gable end. It's a remarkable addition to the level of devotion and adoration that has emanated from the Blackpool supporters down the years. Supporters who, through the generations, have had the opportunity and honour to watch the likes of Jimmy Hampson, Stan Mortensen, Stanley Matthews, Alan Ball, Tony Green and Charlie Adam. The fact that Jimmy has a popularity level that goes beyond all of those great players is a tribute to his total loyalty to the town he always loved.

Tragically, the disease he had fought so hard against and beaten, came back for another battle in 2016 and, sadly, Jimmy wasn't strong enough this time. Despite his brave and courageous words, he was not able to fight anymore. He spent the last few days of his life in Trinity Hospital, Blackpool – a place he'd actually been instrumental in setting up many years before. He was surrounded by his family and the story is that one of the last things he said was that the only regret he had was that he wanted to play one last game of football. It said so much about him. He died on the 22 January 2018.

The tributes followed very quickly from a grieving football world. Sir Bobby Charlton, who had known Jimmy on and off the pitch for decades, and who was a friend, as well as a playing colleague, said:

> As an opponent, team-mate and friend he was, without doubt, one of the most honest and genuine gentlemen I had the good fortune to meet. I have missed listening to his authoritative radio commentaries and now I will miss seeing Mr Blackpool around the scene.

Sir Geoff Hurst, who had played in the England team with him as part of the build-up to the 1966 World Cup, said:

> Jimmy was a great part of our group at the World Cup, one of the great full-backs and one of the nicest guys you could wish to meet. I got to know him more after the World Cup, playing golf and at the reunions. Just an absolutely super guy and a sad loss.

Howard Wilkinson, who had played a part with Jimmy at the FA in helping to find a new England manager and in the implementation of the new training centre at Burton-upon-Trent, said:

> Jimmy's contribution to the game at so many levels is immeasurable. Despite the pressures, success at any price never became an option for Jimmy. He epitomised the beautiful game in thought and deed. A true gentleman.

Former England international and BBC TV presenter Gary Lineker said:

> He was a wonderful footballer and England captain who went on to be a terrific broadcaster of the game he loved, and, most importantly, he was a delightful man. He'll be much missed.

It wasn't just football that paid tribute. Reverend Nicholas Reade, the retired Bishop of Blackburn had this to say at the news of Jimmy's death:

> I am so sad today – Jimmy Armfield was one of the first people to welcome me to the diocese when I arrived in 2004 and I will always remember his warm smile and warm handshake; his hospitality and generosity. His Christian faith was very important to him and helped him through the difficult times as well as the good times.

The tributes came from all over the world and, of course, from his home town of Blackpool. A minute's silence was due to be observed at the next home match but the game was called off due to the weather in a supremely bad piece of timing. There was a memorial held inside the ground and fans also left scarves at the foot of his statue. The club was in a crisis beyond believability at the time, as the fans were boycotting home matches in an attempt to remove the Oyston family from control, something they eventually succeeded in doing. Sadly, Jimmy wasn't alive to see the now famous 'homecoming' game against Southend United in March 2019 when an Oyston-free Blackpool welcomed a capacity crowd of celebrating tangerine-clad supporters, who then witnessed a poor, if not entertaining, 2-2 draw. Somewhere up above, though, you could sense that Jimmy was watching with a smile on his face.

Chapter 27:

The man ...

WHEN YOU write a biography, you try to get as close to the person as possible. What made them what they became? How did they behave? What were their good and what were their bad points? It's not always easy. No one has lived a blameless life but there is nothing that I have seen that is capable of dimming the lustre of the sparkle that Jimmy Armfield had in his life. I can honestly say that, in all the years that I knew him, either watching him play or working alongside him, I never heard a single person have a single bad word to say about him. Also, I never heard Jimmy refer to anyone in a disparaging way. Maybe it was the pre-social media era he was brought up in when people were taught to respect other human beings? Maybe it was through the privations of a relatively poverty-driven childhood, where making sure there was food on the table was of far more importance than the latest celebrity gossip? Maybe, though, it was just the measure of the man.

My first memory of Jimmy Armfield was of him running down the right wing at Bloomfield Road in his tangerine shirt. Yes, I honestly remember that as I was stood in the East

Stand (locally known as the Scratching Sheds for reasons not important here) but I don't remember who we played or what the score was. I remember seeing him at Bloomfield Road as a manager, but for the opposition. He walked along the touchline to the dugout, resplendent in the typical manager's sheepskin coat and sat on the opposition bench as we were playing Bolton Wanderers. He received a great ovation. Down the years, I'd cross paths with him in press rooms and boxes as my BBC career was stuttering into life and, yes, this included the moment he shouted out for everyone to be quiet as he was about to report on 'national radio'. It was said in jest but it registered as everyone immediately stopped talking. Later, I became his producer and spent many happy moments at football grounds where the topic of conversation was nearly always Blackpool's poor form.

The last time I saw Jimmy was in the hospitality lounge at Bloomfield Road on a Friday night. We were there to honour my dear friend, David Oates, who had passed away. He came up to me and asked how I was. In a moment of stunning stupidity, I replied that I was fine but felt very old at that moment.

'Old? No lad. You're not old. You've a way to go yet. I'm old ...' and he smiled. I called him a few years later on the phone, at a time when I'd somehow managed to lose contact with a lot of my former BBC colleagues, and we had a lovely conversation. It was clear he was tired, though, and his voice was weak. I didn't speak to him again.

We all have our memories and the rest of this chapter will be devoted to those who have them, too, but I have a few personal ones. The speeding in Belgium was definitely a highlight for me, as I was being told off by him, but my favourite was when

I called him and asked if he would write a foreword for my new book on Blackpool. Of course he would, and would the cheque be in the post? I hesitated as I hadn't given payment a moment's thought, much to my shame. Then he laughed. He was kidding. The words arrived via email, and they were perfect.

There are two sporting gentlemen who have played a part in my life, where they have entirely enriched my experience just by being there. One was the great Murray Walker, who was one of the most entertaining and funniest of work colleagues, years after I used to listen to his BBC commentaries on Formula One, and, of course, the other is Jimmy. Both are missed and in Blackpool and the footballing world, Jimmy is missed immensely.

The following pages have a selection of tributes and eulogies to Jimmy from many different people from many different walks of life. They are in no specific order and are random but a lot of them are just kind words about the man at different stages of his life. The first is from former Leeds United player Gordon McQueen, who Jimmy took time to speak to after he was sent off in the European Cup semi-final, knowing he wouldn't be able to play in the final. Jimmy did this *while* the game was still being played:

> I was suspended for the final because I'd been sent off for a rush of blood in the semi-final against Barcelona. The following Saturday, against Burnley, I got sent off again. You can imagine how a lot of managers would have reacted, especially as one of my suspensions was for a European Cup Final, but it didn't seem to bother

Jimmy at all. Or, if it did, he never showed it. He just took me aside after the Burnley game and said, 'You'll learn from this.' That stayed with me. He was really good to me, lovely in fact, and I always remember how nice he was to my mum and dad whenever they came to Elland Road. Things like that matter, even to a young swashbuckling defender!

Just a few yards away from the ground and the statue that stands proudly outside the Armfield Stand, is the Armfield Club. A few years ago, it was renovated from its original working men's club state, renamed and refitted. There is also a huge mural on the gable end, showing a smiling Jimmy in his tangerine shirt, with young supporters waving at him. The obvious question was, why Jimmy?

Jimmy's playing days had ceased before people of our age group really started following Blackpool. His name was, however, always revered amongst our elders, not only for his years as a player for Blackpool and England but also for his strong connection with the local community. When a group us got together in 2021 with the objective of creating a supporters' club, the name we considered most fitting was Armfield. When we spoke with the family, we were delighted when they agreed we could use it. The club was opened in October 2020 by one of Jimmy Armfield's sons, John, who made a terrific speech. During his speech, John mentioned that Jimmy was a man of the people who, as a player, chose to walk to matches and stayed loyal to Blackpool FC even when the big clubs came calling. For us, Jimmy's spirit lives on through all who knew and respected him and he still personifies the greatest human virtues of decency, humility and kindness. The Armfield Club was created by Blackpool supporters for Blackpool supporters and we hope it becomes an institution everybody connected with Blackpool can be proud of.

Many people came into Jimmy's life, whether as players, managers or journalists. One of the latter was a man called Dave Edmundson, someone I knew from my days at BBC Radio Lancashire. This is his memory:

The conversation would go something like this.

JA: 'Nice to meet you. Which paper are you from? If you're a reporter, you must be quite good at English?'

Reporter – obvious reply. Name of paper or, as it was in my case, the radio station, because I was a Jimmy A victim.

And usually the response from us all that we thought we were at least competent in writing good English.

'Okay then. Can you write me a sentence that has five consecutive "ands" in it?' i.e. the conjunction.

And Jimmy would walk away. 'If you can't do it, I'll give you the answer at full time.'

Of course, the task appears to be impossible.

Until Jimmy strolled over and gave you the answer.

The end of an era. The final game for Blackpool in 1971.

Rolling the Bloomfield Road grass. Jimmy with Jimmy Kelly, Sammy Salt, Tommy Garrett and Roy Gratrix.

Training in March of 1961

Warm-up completed at Highbury in 1954. Blackpool went on to win 4-1.

Gentleman Jim showing his style. He always made sure he dressed smartly.

Jimmy was well known enough to have a cartoon tribute made for him.

There is always time for an autograph. A lucky fan in the 1968/69 season.

Warming up in the 1958/59 season. A classic Blackpool shirt too.

Jimmy and Anne. A lifetime of happiness.

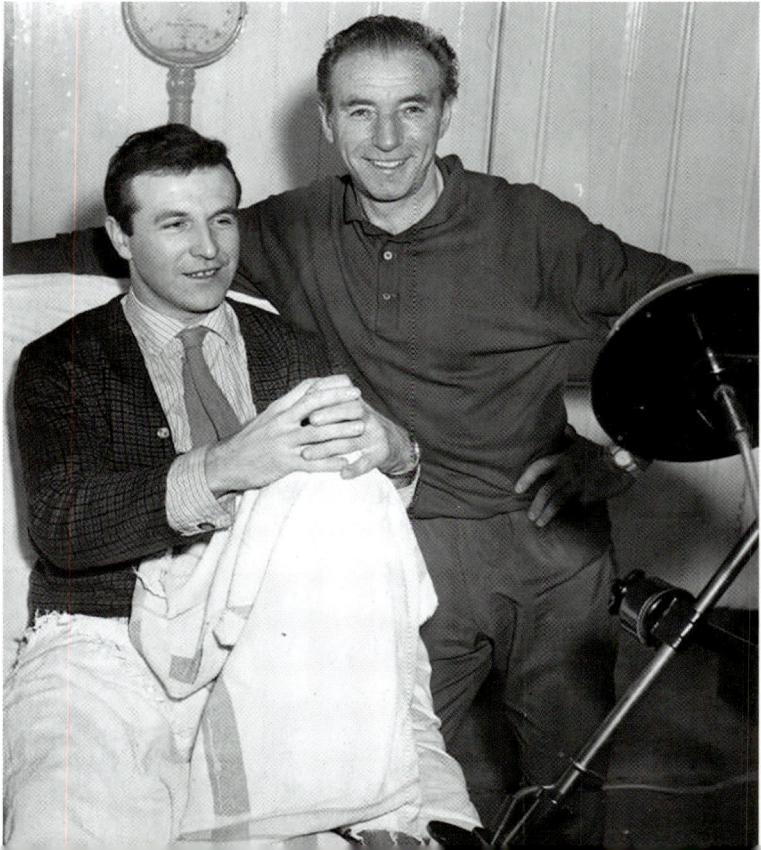

Jimmy recovering in hospital from injury, helped by his great friend and mentor, Stanley Matthews.

Blackpool FC on a tour of the Pacific in the summer of 1958. With Jimmy are Barry Martin, Ray Charnley and Bill Perry.

It's hard being a footballer. Waikiki Beach in Honolulu. It looks like fun, but Jimmy was there for work! Part of a tour of New Zealand.

Away at Birmingham City in 1968. The following season Fred Pickering would join Jimmy at Blackpool.

This is training 1950s style. Run up and down the steps of the Kop until you collapse!

Jimmy has just scored an equaliser against Leicester. He was ecstatic, but later received the wrath of Stanley Matthews for his celebrations.

1967, and his old team-mate Stan Mortensen is the manager of Blackpool now. Ray Charnley shares a joke.

Away to Tottenham Hotspur in August 1965. Despite Jimmy's attempt to stop Spurs scoring, the home side ran riot 4-0.

'There are two professional decorators repainting the pub sign "The Bull and Bush". One of the painters up the ladder, having just finished the brush work, shouts down to his mate "Does that look okay to you?" "No," replies his mate, looking up at the pub sign. "The gaps between The Bull and and and and and Bush are not the same."

Chris Hull, a Blackpool supporter and broadcaster, is someone who knew Jimmy well, especially from his days working at the Football Association. He writes this emotional tribute to his former friend:

Jimmy was, to Blackpool fans, like the royal family is to the country. He provided stability, leadership, inspiration, serenity, honour and grace. I will always remember him attending my dad's funeral, our weekly chats and the gentle life guidance he always offered without preaching. 'Remember, Chris, ultimately life is all about people and the love you put into the world.' Jimmy Armfield will never be forgotten. One of the classiest, most wise and respected footballers and gentlemen of all time. Blackpool's greatest ambassador. Personally, the most unforgettable moment of Jimmy's funeral, which still brings a lump to my throat today, is when I think of the words by his son at the service. Just a few days before Jimmy's passing, he was very poorly and beckoned his son to his bedside and held his hand. As his son got closer, Jimmy – who played a record

627 times for our beloved Blackpool and 43 caps for England – said: 'You know, I wish I could play just one more time.' If a man as great as Jimmy – who reached the very pinnacle of the game – can say that, what a message that is to every young footballer and everyone in the world. Squeeze every drop of goodness and fun out of every opportunity, every match and every day while we still have the chance. Words worth carrying.

I was privileged that Jimmy allowed me to organise his 80th birthday with the fans – 500 places in the Tower Ballroom going in less than one day. Just a couple of weeks before that landmark birthday, I picked up the phone to Jimmy. Just to see how he was doing and chat about the game, as we would do often. Jim was as friendly, wise, engaging and warm as ever. I asked Jimmy in that conversation if there were any plans – other than obvious family ones – to celebrate his 80th birthday, which was around a fortnight away. Jimmy said there weren't any, so I asked him if he would mind if I put together an 80th birthday celebration for the fans and his football friends to attend. Jimmy's typically humble response was, 'I don't think anyone would be interested?' Just over four weeks later, with the brilliant help of everyone at Blackpool Tower and the people of Blackpool, the famous ballroom was full and Jimmy and his family were celebrated in appropriate fashion. I am deeply honoured that Jimmy allowed me to organise and host that landmark celebration for him. I am also thrilled that we managed to get Jimmy to perform in front of the public on the world famous Wurlitzer on that night for the first and only time. Jimmy will always mean the world to Blackpool fans. His legacy was assured a long time ago. He will never be forgotten. I said on that Monday morning when I heard the very sad news of Jimmy's passing, 'A genuine legend of the game and his beloved Blackpool community has left us today. I believe Jimmy Armfield is the greatest all round football person of all-time. One-club man, England captain, manager, football ambassador, broadcaster, writer and, mostly, gentleman.' I feel that even stronger today. Blackpool and the game are so much poorer without Jimmy Armfield in the world, who served it for over eight decades.

I wrote these words below for a speech to Jimmy, his family and the guests on the night of his birthday celebration at the Tower Ballroom. I hope they still resonate. 'An 80th birthday dinner and celebration with Blackpool and England football legend Jimmy Armfield CBE: Thursday, 22 October 2015, Blackpool Tower Ballroom. As we sit in the glorious surroundings of the historic ballroom at The Blackpool Tower, I can think of no better setting to host Jimmy Armfield's 80th birthday celebration. Blackpool's most iconic symbol stands immediately above us, Blackpool's most iconic ambassador sits amongst us. Tonight, however, is more than just celebrating Jimmy the football man and the 43 caps for England, captaining his country 15 times, 627 games for Blackpool over 17 years, respected broadcaster, football official, ambassador of the game, PFA representative and a loyal one-club man. This is about joyously celebrating an incredible landmark for Jimmy the "town of Blackpool man" and the "man of our community" – a man who just gets the most important things in life like public service, giving to others, making a difference, contribution to society and engaging with people. Jimmy is one of the greatest servants to our town and to football. I am honoured he has accepted this invitation to be with us tonight with his family, playing colleagues and friends. We simply couldn't allow the recent wonderful 80th birthday of our friend to go by without showing him that he is still respected and loved as much as ever by the town he has served faultlessly for generations.

'There are few people like Jimmy in the world of football who have served with such distinction in so many areas of the game we love for so long – and they don't celebrate their 80th birthday every year! As Blackpool fans, we are rightly so proud that Jimmy commands respect around the world and that he talks so glowingly of his love for the town of Blackpool everywhere he goes. Have we ever had a greater ambassador for the town than James Christopher Armfield? Will we ever have one like him again? Already, I think we probably have the answer to those questions. So, it is our privilege to celebrate and cherish Jim this evening in the presence of his wonderful wife and lifelong support, Anne, his sons and family. Tonight is a chance for us to listen to

Jimmy's thoughts and experiences of the town, game and country he has served all his life over eight decades – surrounded by his friends and colleagues.

'I am sure many of you share my view that the name Jimmy Armfield is still one of the most important and powerful things in the world of football. There are few who quite understand the sense of serving as Jimmy has, giving all his life at so many different levels with such class. From his debut for the Seasiders as a 19-year-old away at Portsmouth's Fratton Park in 1954 to the inventor of the famous football overlap, his debut for England in the Maracanã against Brazil and Pelé in 1959 in front of 160,000, the greatest right-back accolade at the World Cup in 1962, voted for many seasons in the 1960s as the greatest full-back in Europe, his final game for Blackpool and guard of honour against Manchester United in 1971, an inaugural member of football's playing and coaching Hall of Fames, 2012 FA Cup Final guest of honour – Jimmy has set standards on the field that will be admired forever.

Those are just a few honours of Jim's incredible football playing prowess but off the pitch he is also as an ambassador of the game, football journalist and BBC broadcaster for over 35 years – and still going strong and as insightful as ever. Jim is a supreme analyst of the game, much more than a mere pundit. A gentle authority. Also, he is a vastly respected PFA official and previous anointer of England managers. But it is Jimmy's significant roles within normal life and the community that tell us equally all we need to know about this incredible man. Former high sheriff of Lancashire, current president of Trinity Hospice, president of Age UK – among many other charitable roles and society contributions. At 80, he still also plays the organ at St Peter's C of E Church near Bloomfield Road every Sunday for the congregation. Indeed, the reverence and respect we have for Jimmy is also on a much higher, almost spiritual level. Jimmy, you are 80 years young and you continue to be an inspiration. We wish you many more great birthdays and many more great days! You are an unparalleled gentleman of the town and the game. Sincere best wishes to you Jimmy, your family and to every guest here tonight. God bless, Jimmy, always.'

Steve Wilson was a former colleague at BBC Radio 5 Live and shared the commentary box with Jimmy on many occasions. He has fond memories:

You never quite knew what you might end up talking about off-air when you worked with Jimmy Armfield. Certainly, he was the only man to have captained England's football team who was as likely to recall his organ playing at St Peter's Church in Blackpool the previous Sunday as he was to recall playing behind Sir Stanley Matthews on one of countless sharply remembered Saturdays.

His career as a player was stellar. Recalled to the England squad as captain by Alf Ramsey in the spring of 1966, who knows what part he might have played that glorious summer but for a broken toe sustained against Finland just two weeks before the World Cup finals began?

Who knows where his managerial career might have taken him had his Leeds team won the European Cup Final of 1975 rather than lose a poorly refereed match to the great Bayern Munich of Franz Beckenbauer and Gerd Müller?

When, in 1993, England needed a new manager to replace Graham Taylor they turned to Jimmy to find one. The FA recognised that he had the knowledge, the contacts and the integrity to find the right man. All this, and countless awards, might have made Jimmy proud of his place in the game. In fact, the man who walked out at Wembley shoulder to shoulder with Alfredo di Stéfano also walked the promenades of Blackpool with a humility and grace which surely few such celebrated men could match.

If his career brought him pleasure rather than pride, then Jimmy certainly was fiercely proud of Blackpool – the town whose football club he had represented for two decades.

I remember when the decision was taken to move the National Football Museum from its place at Preston North End's Deepdale Stadium to the centre of Manchester, he was genuinely deeply puzzled.

'Why would they not move it to Blackpool?' he asked. The same might have been said for the national stadium, National Opera, National Theatre and Buckingham Palace.

Many will remember him for his work on BBC Radio and that's where I met him. He should be considered as one of the great voices of sports broadcasting, as influential as Bryon Butler and Peter Jones. Jimmy's co-commentary was such a joy to listen to, so technically perfect and so disciplined. He never talked across his fellow commentator, knowing exactly when to contribute and when to leave gaps. When I think about it, Jimmy Armfield's voice was, in fact, exactly like Jimmy Armfield the man – gentle, avuncular, authoritative and sadly missed.

The fans loved him, which I think has been made obvious in the pages of this book. So, let's hear from two more. The first is Kevin Swales and the second, a former BBC colleague of mine, Paul Burrell:

Jim was a stalwart of Blackpool and Fylde NUJ and a regular at branch meetings in the 1990s when I first started on the Blackpool Gazette. It was always a challenge to get people to come to meetings but Jim rarely missed any. In those days, I think he was writing for the *Sunday Express*. He was a great man of principle and was always standing up for freelance members when the nationals were trying to cheat them. I was a big Pool fan, having seen his final season, and, as a defender, he was my role model. I remember being really in awe of him at branch meetings and was far too starstruck to speak to him or even ask for his autograph. I was so proud that he was a strong union guy with a real sense of justice. I'm proud to say he was part of the branch meeting that approved my NUJ membership.

Last time I saw Jim was the day of the Brexit result when the football museum in Manchester was launching its 1966 World Cup anniversary exhibition. He was chatting to Rob Bonnet of BBC Sport and some other hacks. I have a feeling he had just been diagnosed with cancer for a second time, as he didn't look well. He mentioned in passing he had been for some tests the day before and, by the look on his wife's face, it hadn't been good. But he was in great form, teasing Rob and the assembled hacks. I got a couple of quotes for a feature I was doing.

By the way, Jim wrote some pretty perceptive columns for the *Blackpool Gazette* during the World Cup. He predicted how it would expand and how the African nations would be more prominent. The microfiche of those papers is still in Blackpool Central Library. My first Pool match was Jim's testimonial. I was also at his last one against Man Utd on a day marred by Manc hooligans invading the pitch at the end of the game.

I have really had two heroes growing up in Blackpool. One was 'Sir' Jimmy Armfield, the other was my dad.

Everyone who ever came across Jimmy Armfield would always comment that he was a gentleman. And, when it comes to my father, the one universal comment that comes from practically everyone that knew him was that he was a gentleman, too. I will never forget the day when my father finally found himself face-to-face, great man to great man, in a suite at Blackpool FC. My dad thrust his hand forward and said to Sir Jimmy, 'May I shake your hand, sir?' The two greatest men in my life had met! I'm not sure of the year, I was maybe 15, but Jimmy was in the old supporters' club in the south-western corner. I asked him if I could take a photo of him with my little cheap Brownie camera and immediately he came out of the club and posed for me with no rush whatsoever. Different to Jimmy Greaves, who told me to 'piss off' when, as an eight-year-old, I asked him for his autograph. Also, Tony Waiters, who told me he was not a player when he got on the team bus at a motorway service station when we were all on our way to an away game. That's what always set Jimmy apart from other players as far as I was concerned.

On 8 February 2018, Jimmy Armfield's funeral took place at St Peter's Church, the place that was so close to his heart and the church where he had played the organ virtually every Sunday. It was a private ceremony, attended by the likes of Sir Bobby Charlton, his brother Jack, Sir Trevor Brooking, Gordon Taylor and the Blackpool manager of the time, Gary Bowyer. It was broadcast back to Bloomfield Road for fans to listen to and, indeed, the cortege had driven a lap of the pitch before moving to the church. It was emotional and it was a fitting tribute to a man who had served the town and its football club so well. With the kind permission of his sons, Duncan and John, I have reproduced the speech they gave to say goodbye to their loving father. It hasn't been changed, as that would not be my right to do such a thing, so here it is in its entirety:

Chapter 28:

Dad

'GOOD AFTERNOON everyone and thank you all for attending this celebration of Dad's wonderful life. Many know of his more public life, so John and I will try and describe what he meant to us as a family, especially that special father and son relationship we have.

'Losing Dad is one of the most difficult things I have gone through. As I am standing up here today, I realise how fortunate I was to have him as my dad. There are no words to express his influence in my life. It is through his example that I learned to be the dad, husband and person that I am today, much to the annoyance of my family at times. I think everyone in here who knew him could say that somehow and in some way, he had impacted on their lives in a positive way. That was Dad.

'Many of the messages we have received have told us how he was a second father to them and those random acts of kindness that touched so many lives. He had that gift of knowing when to listen, when to give the words of wisdom and when to just be there at those difficult times.

'He saw being rich, not in terms of how much money people had – in fact, it was not important – but in so many other ways, such as being surrounded by and spending time with family, friends or work colleagues, being happy, fulfilment, helping others and being lucky enough doing something you love. This helped us all to view the world in the same way and why he viewed loyalty as so important. This loyalty manifested itself in many ways, including being married for 60 years (he always said "us Armfield men are a great catch"), being a one-club man and his devotion to his town Blackpool. It was also his patriotism; he was absolutely truthful when he stated that his own personal inclusion in the England team that won the 66 World Cup was a distant second to the fact we won it.

'Dad was hardworking, selfless, strong, honest, kind, loving and gentle. He had no ego and always seemed, as he described, "happy with his lot". He was at total peace with himself and what he had done with his life, although in his final weeks he regretted not buying that new Mercedes or Jaguar.

'He was a modest man. He was showered with awards, which he was deeply flattered by, but it never went to his head. He rang me one day and I could hardly hear him because there was traffic noise and people talking. So, I asked him to speak up and, in a joyful voice, he told me he had been awarded the CBE. I was so pleased for him, so warmly congratulated him on this news and how proud I was of him, but I asked him where he was, as I could hardly hear him? "I am at the bus stop near Highfield Road and Harrowside," came the reply. "Why are you there, Dad?" "I am waiting for the bus to take me to church to practice the organ. You know I've got my bus pass now!"

'He loved his two visits to the palace with his family to get the OBE and CBE and we were blessed to see him receive them. This was true, also, when he became deputy lieutenant of Lancashire, a lay canon and lord high sheriff of Lancashire, with his shield still hanging in Lancaster Castle and our house. His motto on that shield is "persevere", a word that meant a lot to him. He sent me a letter once, after some difficulties I had been having, in which he basically told me this: "Keep going, don't give up; sometimes it's just time for a change." Oh, how true those words were and how right things do turn out when you least expect if you persevere.

'Dad was always interested and proud of my work and achievements and quizzed me often about it. When I travelled in the UK or abroad, each time he would have an interesting fact or story to tell on every location. He was always concerned about how I was being treated, the hours of work I put in and I definitely got my work ethic from him and Mum. He said, "Us Armfields, we are grafters." Dad was never that hands-on father and, whether I wanted it or not, I would get his opinion, usually starting with "now if I were you, this is what I would do".

'He would reminisce and tell stories about his youth. How he experienced real poverty and the hardships of being brought up in an inner city in the late 1930s and the start of the Second World War. Of being evacuated and separated from his beloved father on and off for five years and of moving and living in a one-roomed flat on Tyldesley Road in a new town, Blackpool. He often put all his ailments down to not having enough food during this time. As many of us experienced, he had plenty of these.

'He would talk about how he would go to play football on the beach or the colosseum bus station with some of his friends, occasionally skipping school to do this, and how he climbed up the drainpipe at Revoe School to the roof to retrieve his only tennis ball, as it was so valuable to him.

'Yet, it was this move to a new town that perhaps had the greatest effect on his future and an affinity developed.

'He came to love Blackpool and said this as often as he could to anyone who would listen. Whatever he was doing in his life, the draw of Blackpool was too great and he never left. This meant turning down many lucrative jobs in football, hours and hours of extra travelling when a simple house move or overnight stay would have made his life simpler. He always said to me the reason for the travelling was to have the satisfaction of returning to his beloved Blackpool, his home.

'It is here his parents settled after the war. He met the love of his life, my mother. He made many friends, he represented its football team, he learned to be a journalist, he put down his roots, he watched with real pride as his family grew and prospered, he worked tirelessly for the betterment of the community, he experienced good and bad times. In short, Dad and Blackpool became totally intertwined – being rewarded as a freeman of the borough.

'This church, St Peter's, has been a large part of Dad's life from being a small boy when Burt Ellis first brought him here. It was one of the great family events of the week. Sunday morning off to church, Dad playing the organ, Mum singing or both of them running the Sunday school, growing the numbers so large the church hall wasn't really big enough. Then off to

Woodhead's garage for petrol and a chat with Arthur and Peter and, finally, to grandparents for Sunday lunch and treats.

'I feel he also felt close to nature and God when he was in his garden, pottering around, growing his geraniums from cuttings and battling moss on his lawn. A passion for his garden came from his father, Chris. He regularly got John and me to pick up topsoil for him and, when we were children, he forced us to follow the horses and donkeys on the promenade to pick up manure. "There is nothing like the fresh stuff," he would say. "No straw in it." And there certainly wasn't!

'Dad believed in lifelong learning. He would often say to me, "Learn from every experience you have." He believed in social mobility and that everyone has to be given the opportunity to develop their talents. I remember one day I was training as a youth team player at Manchester United. On a Friday, there used to be a five-a-side competition where all players and staff played. One week, Dad came along and was invited to play. Two minutes into the first game, the ball broke to him ten yards out from my goal. Out I flew to close the space, only to see him chip the ball over me into the net. No celebration for Dad. He just looked me in the eye and said, "I've told you before … stay on your feet as long as you can and watch the ball, not the player."

'Those opportunities he experienced and grabbed, he felt everyone should be given a chance to do the same. I think this is why he worked towards this with the Prince's Trust, Outward Bound, being a governor at Arnold School and his work at the PFA. Again, he selflessly gave his time just to see these institutions succeed in this quest. His generosity extended to all the charity work he did, giving his time freely to help support those things close to his heart, such as the hospice and Help the Aged.

'He was offered a university place prior to going to do his National Service. The Korean War was on but he always joked that the furthest east he went was Catterick as a PE instructor. However, the experience shaped him and he met and played football with many of his lifelong friends.

'Who were the biggest influences in his life? Well, there was not one individual, as he felt everyone he came into contact with had made their mark on him. There are a few that perhaps stand out in his early years. His grandfather ("the old fellow"); his parents; Frank Holgate, the headmaster at Arnold School; Joe Smith, his first manager at Blackpool, Stan Matthews, who he played behind for five years; Walter Winterbottom, his first England manager.

'Dad had time for everyone and was a man of the people. I remember him telling me that, when he first broke into the Blackpool team, on home matchdays he would wait for his friends to call for him and they would walk as part of the matchday crowd from his home in Bairstow Street to Bloomfield Road, sharing a laugh and a joke, at the same time delivering groceries for his father to boarding houses on the way, before splitting up at the ground – Dad to the changing rooms to play in the old First Division and his friends to watch in the crowd.

'When he set his mind on achieving something, he had the ability to push himself and maximise his potential. He never felt he was gifted like many others. Hard work and honesty with himself was the key. He told me he felt he struggled defending crosses at the back post; well, I suppose anyone would with the likes of Nat Lofthouse tearing in from behind you. Dad's solution? To spend an hour each afternoon after training heading crosses away. When he wanted to visit the rest of his family in Manchester and money was short, he would cycle the 47 miles on a shop bike similar to the one used by Granville in *Open All Hours*, sometimes going there and back in a day. He loved that TV show, as he said it reminded him of his days working with his father in his grocer's shop.

'They say behind every great man, there has to be a great woman, and that was Mum. The love of Dad's life, they first met as children at Revoe School, starting to share their love of music by Polish dancing and singing together. Then later, during their "courting" phase, there were frequent rendezvous at the Tower Ballroom, dancing the night away and listening to that Wurlitzer organ. They were married in June 1958 at Chappel Street Methodist Church, moving into a club house at Ravenwood Avenue. In this house, Dad built a garage with Mum's Uncle Teddy. In those days, the rent was deducted from his pay and Dad found out it had mysteriously gone up, so he went to see the club secretary to ask why. "Well, you have a garage now, so more rent." "Yes, but I paid for it," said Dad. "Not my problem," was the reply ... so it stayed at that higher level!

'Mum supported Dad and was the glue that held the family together, especially when Dad went off to play abroad, in those days for weeks at a time. After the playing days, Mum went to virtually every social event, including that hectic year when Dad was lord high sheriff and his commitments to charity and work. They were devoted to each other and shared so many passions, including music, the church, the local community and the love of the family.

'Dad was so proud of you, Mum, being by his side and rock for all those wonderful years and, as Dad's health was failing, it was that special love and care only you, Mum, could give that kept him going so long.

'Dad was a man of habits. Some would say eccentricities. He had a series of quotes that he would use to defend his lifestyle and decisions. When his family used to question what he was wearing or why he wouldn't replace items in and around the house, he would reply with one of his favourites: "They are plenty good enough for me." When Mum went to make everyone a warm drink, when asked, he would always say: "No, I'm all right." Then, when Mum was bringing in the drinks, he would say: "Go on then, I'll have half a cup." It didn't mean any extra work for Mum, as she would have already made it, knowing he would change his mind, but many others were caught out by this. It was hard to watch without commenting as your dad rode off wearing an old tracksuit on an old-fashioned red bike with a red saddle to do the shopping but he would always reply with more of his favourites: "Don't worry about me, worry about yourself," or "No one will notice me, as they are busy looking at themselves."

'Right to the end, he remained the same. He still had his cheeky smile, a glint in his eye and his sense of humour and, when asked if he wanted a brew, smirked and said, "Go on then, I'll just have half a cup."

'Of course, playing or being around football, including broadcasting, was a way of life. He would have done this for nothing, as he saw it as being rich. A few weeks ago, he was lying in bed, as he was unwell, and I was with him. I was holding his hands and talking about the family and I think he knew at this stage things were not great in terms of his health, so we discussed what lay ahead. All of a sudden, he stopped, lifting his head up to look me in the eye and said, "You know, Duncan, I wish I could play football one more time." I said, "I wish you could as well, Dad." We shared a tear.

He loved his family and was deeply devoted to my mother, Anne; her family; his parents, Chris and Doris; my brother, Duncan, and his wife, Deborah; Julie, my wife; his four grandchildren, James, Tom, Nick and Hannah; and other members of the family.

Dad
I will miss your smile
I will miss that voice
I will miss those wise words
I will miss our chats
I will miss your humour
Most of all, I will miss you Dad … but I know you will always be with me and that's why I love you.
I really loved my dad.'

God bless Jimmy Armfield. May he always rest in peace.

Statistics

Playing career – Blackpool 1954–1971

Debut – 27 December 1954 – Portsmouth 3 Blackpool 0 (First Division) attendance 43,896. Fratton Park

Final appearance – 1 May 1971 – Blackpool 1 Manchester United 1 (First Division) attendance 29,857. Bloomfield Road

1954/55 – 2 league appearances, 0 goals.

1955/56 – 30 league appearances, 1 FA Cup appearance, 0 goals.

1956/57 – 38 league appearances, 4 FA Cup appearances, 0 goals.

1957/58 – 28 league appearances, 1 FA Cup appearance, 0 goals.

1958/59 – 32 league appearances, 6 FA Cup appearances, 0 goals.

1959/60 – 41 league appearances, 3 FA Cup appearances, 1 goal.

1960/61 – 40 league appearances, 1 FA Cup appearance, 1 league Cup appearance, 0 goals.

1961/62 – 37 league appearances, 2 FA Cup appearances, 6 League Cup appearances, 0 goals.

1962/63 – 39 league appearances, 2 FA Cup appearances, 2 League Cup appearances, 0 goals.

1963/64 – 35 league appearances, 2 FA Cup appearances, 2 League Cup appearances, 0 goals.

1964/65 – 40 league appearances, 1 FA Cup appearance, 1 League Cup appearances, 2 goals.

1965/66 – 35 league appearances, 2 FA Cup appearances, 2 League Cup appearances, 1 goal.

1966/67 – 29 league appearances, 0 FA Cup appearances, 2 League Cup appearances, 0 goals.

1967/68 – 41 league appearances, 2 FA Cup appearances, 2 League Cup appearances, 1 goal.

1968/69 – 34 league appearances, 1 FA Cup appearance, 4 League Cup appearances, 0 goals.

1969/70 – 40 league appearances, 3 FA Cup appearances, 2 League Cup appearances, 1 goal.

1970/71 – 27 league appearances, 2 FA Cup appearances, 1 League Cup appearance. 0 goals.

Total – 568 league appearances, 33 FA Cup appearances, 25 League Cup appearances, 6 goals.

England Under-23 – 1956–59
Debut – 26 September 1956 – Denmark 0 England 3 (international friendly) – attendance 15–25,000. Copenhagen

Final appearance – 7 May 1959 – Italy 0 England 3 (tour of Europe) – attendance 70–80,000. Milan.

1956/57 – 1 appearance, 0 goals.
1957/58 – 1 appearance, 0 goals.
1958/59 – 4 appearances, 0 goals.

England 'B' – 1957
Debut – 19 May 1957 – Bulgaria 2 England 1 (Iron Curtain tour match) – attendance 55,000. Sofia.

Final appearance – 30 May 1957 – Czechoslovakia 0 England 2 (Iron Curtain tour match) – attendance 22,000. Bratislava.

1956/57 – 3 appearances, 0 goals.

England – 1959–66
Debut – 13 May 1959 – Brazil 2 England 0 (tour of South America) – attendance 150–175,000. Rio de Janeiro.

Final appearance – 26 June 1966 – Finland 0 England 3 (pre-World Cup tour) – attendance 12,899. Helsinki.

1958/59 – 4 appearances, 0 goals.

1959/60 – 4 appearances, 0 goals.

1960/61 – 9 appearances, 0 goals.

1961/62 – 12 appearances, 0 goals (including 4 appearances in the 1962 World Cup finals in Chile)

1962/63 – 8 appearances, 0 goals.

1963/64 – 4 appearances, 0 goals.

1965/66 – 2 appearances, 0 goals.

British Championship (Home Nations Championship) – 13 appearances, 0 goals.

World Cup Finals – 4 appearances, 0 goals.

Total – 43 appearances, 0 goals. Captain on 15 occasions.

Jimmy also made 12 appearances for the Football League between 1956 and 1963.

Management career

Bolton Wanderers 1971-74
First game – 14 August 1971 – Oldham Athletic 2 Bolton Wanderers 2 (Third Division) – Boundary Park.

Last game – 28 September 1974 – Bolton Wanderers 1 Notts County 1 (Second Division) – Burnden Park

1971/72 – P46 W17 D16 L13 F51 A41 PTS50 – 7th position in the Third Division.
FA Cup – Round 4 – 0-3 away to Chelsea.
League Cup – Round 4 replay – 0-6 at home to Chelsea.
1972/73 – P46 W25 D11 L10 F73 A39 PTS61 – Champions of the Third Division.
FA Cup – Round 5 – 0-1 at home to Luton Town.
League Cup – Round 2 – 0-2 at Sheffield Wednesday.
1973/74 – P42 W15 D12 L15 F44 A 40 PTS42 – 11th in the Second Division.
FA Cup – Round 4 replay – 0-2 at home to Southampton.
League Cup – Round 3 replay – 1-2 at home to Millwall.
1974/75 – P8 W2 D2 L4 F7 A9 PTS6
League Cup – Round 2 replay – 1-3 away to Norwich City
Total – P180 W80 D47 L53 – 44.4 win percentage.

Leeds United – 1974–78
First game – 5 October 1974 – Leeds United 2 Arsenal 0 (First Division) – Elland Road.

Last game – 29 April 1978 – Queens Park Rangers 0 Leeds United 0 (First Division) – Loftus Road.

1974/75 – P42 W16 D13 L13 F57 A49 PTS45 – Ninth in the First Division.
FA Cup – Quarter-Final 3rd replay – 2-3 away to Ipswich Town.
League Cup – Round 4 – 0-3 away to Chester City.

European Cup – Final – 0-2 to Bayern Munich.

1975/76 – P42 W21 D9 L12 F65 A46 PTS51 – 5th in the First Division.

FA Cup – Round 4 – 0-1 at home to Crystal Palace.

League Cup – Round 3 – 0-1 at home to Notts County.

1976/77 – P42 W15 D12 L15 F48 A51 PTS42 – 10th in the First Division.

FA Cup – Semi-Finals – 1-2 to Manchester United.

League Cup – Round 1 – 0-1 away to Stoke City.

1977/78 – P42 W18 D10 L14 F63 A53 PTS46 – 9th in the First Division.

FA Cup – Round 3 – 1-2 at home to Manchester City.

League Cup – Semi-Finals – 3-7 aggregate to Nottingham Forest.

Total – P193 W87 D47 L59 – 45.1 win percentage.

Index

S

Scotland U-23 – 56, 150
Scotland National Team – 68, 69, 70, 78, 79, 92, 93, 197
Shankly, Bill – 130
Shannon, Les – 106, 109
Sheffield Wednesday FC – 93, 103
Sheffield United – 154, 204
Shimwell, Eddie – 45
Smith, Joe – 29, 40. 41, 44, 50, 51, 52, 54, 55, 164
Soviet Union National Team – 60
Spain National Team – 69
St. Peter's Church – 27, 205, 230, 234, 239
Stokoe, Bob – 109, 111
Suart, Ron – 55, 87, 104
Switzerland National Team – 92

T

Taylor, Graham – 188, 190, 192, 231
Tottenham Hotspur FC – 32, 42, 191, 193, 194
Tranmere Rovers FC - 163

U

United States National Team – 66, 94
Uruguay National Team – 94, 95

V

Venables, Terry – 191, 192, 193, 194, 196, 196

W

Wales National Team – 68, 69, 79, 91, 93
War Cup – 22, 23, 29,
Wembley Stadium – 54, 59, 60, 61, 68, 73, 75, 78, 79, 89, 90, 91, 93, 98, 100, 102, 103, 147, 174, 176, 195, 196, 211, 213, 231
West Germany National Team – 100
Wilson, Ray – 68
Wilson, Steve - 230
Winterbottom, Walter – 56, 62, 67, 69, 70, 77, 80, 89, 90, 91, 241
World Cup 1962 – 64, 68, 77, 78, 80, 81, 82, 83, 84, 87, 89, 166, 229
World Cup 1966 – 92, 93, 97, 98, 100, 101, 103, 112, 117, 119, 174, 217, 237
Wright, Billy – 64, 66, 67, 68

Y

Young Footballer of the Year – 67
Yugoslavia National Team – 69, 98